THE KOALA

Look for these and other books in the
Lucent Endangered Animals and Habitats series:

The Amazon Rain Forest
The Bald Eagle
The Bear
Birds of Prey
The Cougar
Coral Reefs
The Elephant
The Giant Panda
The Gorilla
The Jaguar
The Manatee
The Oceans
The Orangutan
The Rhinoceros
Seals and Sea Lions
The Shark
Snakes
The Tiger
Turtles and Tortoises
The Whale
The Wolf

Other related titles in the Lucent Overview series:

Acid Rain
Endangered Species
Energy Alternatives
Garbage
The Greenhouse Effect
Hazardous Waste
Ocean Pollution
Oil Spills
Ozone
Pesticides
Population
Rainforests
Recycling
Saving the American Wilderness
Vanishing Wetlands
Zoos

THE KOALA

BY ANN MALASPINA

Endangered
Animals &
Habitats

LUCENT BOOKS, INC.
SAN DIEGO, CALIFORNIA

Library of Congress Cataloging-in-Publication Data

Malaspina, Ann, 1957–
    The koala / by Ann Malaspina.
        p.   cm. — (Endangered animals & habitats)
Includes bibliographical references (p. 92).
    ISBN 1-56006-876-0 (hardback : alk. paper)
    1. Koala—Juvenile literature. 2. Endangered species—Juvenile
literature.   I. Title.   II. Series.
    QB54.R37   1991
    599.2'5—dc21

2001001768

Contents

Introduction

AS THE TWENTY-FIRST century unfolds, the koala's conservation status, or whether the species is threatened with extinction, is controversial. In some parts of its range in south and southeast Australia, human activity is destroying the eucalyptus forests, which the koala relies on for food and habitat, reducing the koala's numbers and putting those that survive at serious risk of starvation and loss of habitat. But in other isolated regions, koala populations have grown too numerous for their home ranges. They are stripping the eucalyptus trees of leaves, causing ecological damage and food shortages.

The two scenarios seem very different: Too few koalas in some places and too many in others. Yet both problems have the same root cause. Destruction of habitat in the koala's historic range throughout Australia has left the ancient tree-living marsupial with fewer places to live. The koala is forced to survive in smaller, more fragmented woodlands, where it may overgraze the food trees or lose food and habitat altogether.

Today, most koalas share their habitat, in one way or another, with humans. Koalas are found wandering along roads after being injured by cars. They fall into suburban swimming pools and are attacked by domestic dogs. In rural areas, they share land with grazing livestock, which can harm their food trees. They compete with loggers for trees in state forests. "Our impact on koala populations is immense and in some ways immeasurable. Koalas do not occupy our backyards, we have moved into theirs,"[1] writes

Ann Sharp, general manager of the Australian Koala Foundation, an information and advocacy group for koalas.

The koala is one of Australia's most beloved and well-known native animals. The image of a koala perched in the branches of a eucalyptus tree is familiar to people around the world. According to a recent study, the koala is critical to the Australian tourism industry, bringing thousands of tourists to the country each year in hopes of glimpsing the animal in the wild. But as one journalist recently observed, the koala has "a high popularity rating and a faltering conservation record."[2]

While there is no official count of koalas in the wild today, their numbers have fallen sharply since the turn of the twentieth century, when the population is estimated to have been in the millions. Hunting the koala for its valuable fur pelt nearly wiped out the species by the 1930s. A public outcry stopped the hunt, and the koala became a protected species.

Koalas huddle together in a eucalyptus tree, their natural habitat.

But as Australia developed rapidly in the next decades, the koala's habitat was destroyed. Logging, farming, grazing, and residential and urban development did not stop to save a eucalyptus tree. Natural phenomena, particularly bush fire and drought, aggravated by human activity, also wiped out many acres of eucalyptus forest.

Today, loss of forests and conflicts with humans are putting the koala at risk in much of its historic range. Estimates of the koala population today range from 40,000 to upwards of 100,000. In New South Wales, a populous state on Australia's east coast, koalas have disappeared from 50 to 75 percent of their former range and are uncommon, rare, or extinct in many parts of the state. These dwindling numbers have led the koala to be classified as a vulnerable species in New South Wales.

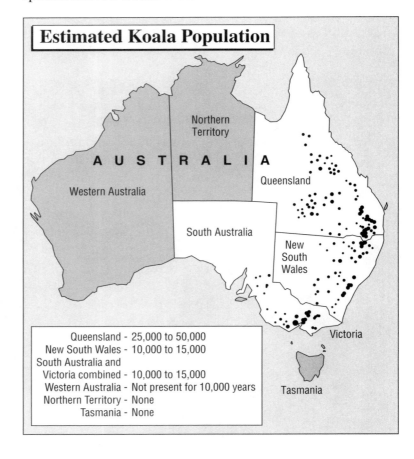

Estimated Koala Population

Northern Territory

A U S T R A L I A

Western Australia

Queensland

South Australia

New South Wales

Victoria

Tasmania

Queensland - 25,000 to 50,000
New South Wales - 10,000 to 15,000
South Australia and
  Victoria combined - 10,000 to 15,000
Western Australia - Not present for 10,000 years
Northern Territory - None
Tasmania - None

Even as many local koala populations decline, others are expanding too rapidly for their available habitat. On Snake Island, a small island southeast of Melbourne, the capital of the state of Victoria, a growing population of some twenty-four hundred koalas is stripping the island's eucalyptus trees of leaves. Wildlife officials say that the island's eucalyptus woodlands can feed only half that number of koalas. Scientists are trying to come up with a plan to save these koalas from starvation.

Protecting the koala

This unusual contrast in the animal's status has led to disagreement over whether the koala needs special protections. Though it is illegal to hunt or harm koalas anywhere in Australia, further protections for the koala and its habitat vary in different parts of the country. Thus far, Australia has determined the koala does not meet the criteria for a nationally endangered or threatened species. The koala was not listed in the Environment Protection and Biodiversity Conservation Act of 1999, which names the Australian animal and plant species that are vulnerable, threatened, or extinct. The listing would allow the government to prohibit the destruction of critical koala habitat and would require a recovery plan for the species. Without national listing, the management of koalas is left primarily to the four (out of six) Australian states with koala populations.

The states, because of different geographies, industries, populations, and natural resources, treat the koala differently. In New South Wales, where the koala was listed as "vulnerable" under the Threatened Species Conservation Act of 1995, some protections exist for koala habitat, requiring development to take into consideration koala populations. To the north of New South Wales, the state of Queensland considers the koala as "common wildlife" under the Nature Conservation (Wildlife) Regulation of 1994, a designation that gives the koala few protections. The koala has no official listing in Victoria, while it is considered "rare" in South Australia.

International concern about the koala is growing. In 1996, the International Union of Conservation of Nature (IUCN)

The koala is currently listed as a "near threatened" species by the International Union of Conservation of Nature.

listed the koala as "near threatened" on its Red List of endangered and threatened species. The Red List reports on threatened and endangered species worldwide. The status of "near threatened" means that the koala could become vulnerable if it continues its current decline in the wild.

After being pressed by Australian and international conservation groups, the U.S. Fish and Wildlife Service in 2000 listed the koala as threatened under the U.S. Endangered Species Act, in part to draw attention to the plight of the koala. But many Australians protested the listing, saying that the koala is not a threatened species nationwide.

Solving the koala's numerous problems will not be easy. Protecting the koala requires people to balance many conflicting issues in Australia, from the rate of timber production in eucalyptus forests to suburban sprawl in historic koala habitat. Still, as scientists learn more about what the koala needs to survive, and how best to manage local populations, there are signs of hope for the ancient marsupial.

1

Life in a Eucalyptus Tree

FOUND NOWHERE ELSE in the wild except in east and southeast Australia, the koala is perfectly suited for life in the region's forests and woodlands. The koala relies on the Australian trees belonging to the genus *Eucalyptus* for both food and habitat. Because the koala is so specialized in where it lives and what it eats, the koala is able to live a long healthy life in a eucalyptus woodland, but it cannot survive easily elsewhere.

Rousing only to forage for leaves to eat, or to scramble down the tree trunk in search of a new tree with a more plentiful leaf supply, the koala spends as much as twenty hours a day dozing in the limbs of a eucalyptus tree. Its teeth are shaped bluntly to gnaw the tough, chewy leaves, while the rough pads on the soles of its feet and palms of its hands help it to grip the smooth, hard tree trunks and branches. Equipped with a good sense of balance, the koala securely wedges itself in tree branches even while asleep.

The koala in a family of its own

Like some 151 Australian mammals, from kangaroos to the hare wallaby, the koala is a marsupial. Although marsupials are mammals, a distinct feature separates them. Most mammals, from humans to whales, have a placenta to nourish their embryos in the womb. Most marsupials have no placenta, or only a very basic placenta like the koala, so that the gestation period is very short. The marsupial female

11

gives birth before the baby, or joey, is fully developed, then nourishes and protects it in an outer pouch.

While koalas share many characteristics with other marsupials, they are sufficiently distinct to be classified as the only member of the scientific family, *Phascolarctidae*. Its scientific name is *Phascolarctos cinereus*, which means ash-colored pouched bear. Some of the koala's distinguishing characteristics include its cheek pouches used to store food

A koala hangs from a tree with her joey safely tucked in her outer pouch.

and the fact that the female's pouch opens toward the tail, in contrast with most other marsupials, whose pouches open in the front.

Scientists have identified three subspecies of the koala. Northern koalas, *P.c. adjustus*, are found in the state of Queensland in northeast Australia. They are small, weighing between eleven and seventeen pounds, with a short coat of silver-gray fur. Southern koalas, *P.c. victor victoria*, are found in the state of Victoria, where the climate is colder. Sometimes twice as large as the Northern koalas, the Southern males grow to about twenty-six pounds, while the females are slightly smaller, at about seventeen pounds. The Southern koalas have a longer, thicker coat of cinnamon-colored fur to shield them from the colder weather. A third subspecies, *P.c. cinereus*, which has grayish fur, was described in 1817 in New South Wales, which lies between Victoria and Queensland.

Clues to the koala's past

Other subspecies of the koala may have existed long ago, as fossil finds have suggested. For example, the fossil of a giant koala, dating back 2 to 5 million years and more than twice the size of the modern koala, was found in southern Australia. Fossils have provided scientists with clues about prehistoric koalas. In 1953, the teeth and jaw fragments of a cousin of the modern koala were found in a site dating back 24 million years in central Australia. These fragments led scientists to believe the earlier koalas also lived in trees and ate tree leaves.

From studies of the shape and structure of fossilized koala teeth, scientists learned that most of the ancient koalas were also herbivores, or plant-eating animals, and ate the same diet of eucalyptus leaves as modern koalas. In fact, this specialized diet allowed the koala to survive as a species when Australia's climate began warming about 12 to 15 million years ago as the island slowly moved closer to the equator. At that time, Australia's climate changed from wet and tropical to hot and dry. While other vegetation died out because of the drier weather, the eucalyptus trees and bushes flourished and spread, enabling the koala to survive into the present day.

The fossil records also provide clues to where koalas once lived. The range of the koala was historically much broader than it is today. Fossil remains of koalas have been found in caves around Perth, Western Australia, and all along the southern coast of Australia, as well as some interior areas. These locations have not seen native koalas in recent history.

A koala is not a bear

When immigrants from Great Britain arrived on the eastern coast of Australia beginning in 1788, they saw a koala for the first time. They mistakenly believed that the furry, roundish animal perched in a tree was a kind of bear, an animal familiar to Europeans. In fact, they had no idea what it was, since there were no koalas in Europe. "They are called by some monkeys, by others bears, but they by no means answer to either species. I first took them to be a species of the Sloth. . . . I now think that these animals most resemble, and come nearest to the loris, or slow-paced lemur of India,"[3] wrote William Govatt, a British surveyor, in 1836. Mystified by the unfamiliar animal, the new settlers did not know what type of species it was—a confusion that persists to the present time.

Even today, some people still call the animal "the koala bear." The koala may look something like a small bear, but the two have almost nothing in common, besides fur and the fact that they are both mammals. Like the bear, appearance can be deceiving. Although the koala may appear soft and cuddly, with its smallish head and large fluffy ears, it is extremely strong and its compact body is lean and muscular.

Its body is suited to the environment in which it lives. The koala's short, soft, springy fur is good insulation from extreme weather. In heavy rainfall, the koala curls in a tight ball, allowing the rain to flow off its dense fur. The koala's fur, whether brown or gray, also offers camouflage in the grayish leaves of the eucalyptus. On the chest, chin, and forelimbs, the koala's fur is white.

Life in the trees

Existing primarily in the limbs of trees, the koala is an arboreal, or tree-living, marsupial. The koala's long limbs are well-designed for an arboreal life. They support the koala's weight while it is climbing, and wrap around the tree limbs for stability when it is at rest. A koala's thigh muscles are thick and strong, which helps it climb tree

 How the Koala Got Its Name

When the Europeans arrived in Australia in the eighteenth century, they did not know what to call the unfamiliar koala. They soon discovered that the Aboriginal people had their own words for the animal. Cullawine, koolewong, colo, colah, koolah, kaola, koala, karbor, boorabee, and goribun were just some of the Aboriginal words for koalas, recorded in writing by early settlers, according to the Australian Koala Foundation.

Some people believe that the word "koala" comes from the language of the Katang, a tribe of Australian aborigines, and means "no water" or "does not drink." Since the koala generally gets its water from the leaves of the eucalyptus tree, this meaning would seem accurate. Yet there were so many different languages spoken by Aboriginal tribes that the word "koala" might have come from somewhere else.

The first European to report sighting a koala was John Price, a free servant of Australia's governor Captain John Hunter. Price was traveling west of Sydney, Australia, in 1798, when he wrote in his diary that he saw "an animal which the natives call a Cullawine, which resembles the sloths of America," as Simon Hunter records in *The Official Koala Handbook*.

A few years later, in 1803, the *Sydney Gazette* newspaper published the first scientific description of a koala, which had been captured by an explorer, Ensign F. Barrallier, and presented to the governor of Australia in Sydney. The newspaper described the koala, in part, as "somewhat larger than a Waumbut [wombat], nevertheless, it differs from that animal," according to Hunter. Still, the newspaper had no name for the animal.

In 1816, the French zoologist Henri-Marie Ducrotay de Blainville gave the koala its scientific family name, *Phascolarctos*, from the Greek words, *Phasco* for "leather pouch" and *larctos* for "bear." At the time, the koala was thought to be a kind of bear. Later, the German naturalist Georg August Goldfuss gave it the specific name, *cinereus*, a Latin word meaning ash-colored. Thus, the scientific name for the koala is *Phascolarctos cinereus*.

trunks. Koalas have long, curved, powerful claws and five-clawed digits on their forepaws. The two first digits of the koala's forepaws are opposed, or separate, from the other three digits. Using its opposing digits, the koala can open its hands widely to securely grip the tree branches. The hind feet are big, with one clawless thumb and the second and third toes fused together. The fused digits are used as a comb for grooming. Both the hands and feet have rough nonslip pads to help the koala grip the tree branches.

To climb a tree, the koala springs from the ground and attaches itself to the bark using its strong, sharp, front claws. Using both hands and feet, the koala bounds up the tree. The koala likes to wedge itself into a fork of the tree so that it will not fall. Amidst the fur, the koala's tail is a barely visible stump, with no apparent function. It was likely longer at some point in the koala's evolution, and scientists speculate that the tail was once used to secure its body on tree branches.

The koala browses through a tree, picking and choosing the leaves it wants to eat. Once it has eaten all the leaves it wants in one tree, it moves to another. The koala descends the tree trunk, then quickly hurries across the ground to the

Koalas have powerful claws, which they use for climbing and gripping tree branches.

nearest available food tree. On the ground, koalas appear to walk awkwardly, using their front right foot, then their back left foot, their front left foot, then their back right foot. But, in fact, they are quite nimble. The koala is able to run when necessary, using both front feet, then both back feet. It is even able to leap and to swim. The koala does not stay on the ground for long, since on the ground it becomes vulnerable to predators and other dangers, such as traffic on the roads. As soon as the koala finds a suitable new tree, it scrambles up.

A treetop branch offers a safe, comfortable place for a koala who sleeps up to eighteen hours a day.

Nocturnal marsupial

The koala spends most of its life high up in the branches of a eucalyptus tree, at rest or asleep for up to eighteen hours a day. As a nocturnal animal, the koala is rarely active during the hours of daylight. When night falls, the koala begins its brief period of activity. Under the cover of darkness, it undertakes its routine behaviors of eating, mating, or moving from tree to tree.

The koala feeds mainly on the leaves of eucalyptus trees.

Because it usually moves relatively slowly on the ground and has no defenses against predators, darkness helps the koala, and especially the young joey, to hide from its enemies in the wild, such as eagles, snakes, and dingos, Australia's native wild dogs. Being nocturnal also allows the koala to live close to human settlements, since its activity takes place when people are asleep, thus reducing conflicts.

A toxic diet

When it wakes at dusk, the koala starts foraging for food, its most important daily undertaking. The koala is a famously picky eater. In scientific terms, the animal is called a specialized browser, which means that it feeds mainly on one type of food, the leaves of the trees in the genus *Eucalyptus*. Of the hundreds of species of eucalyptus trees and bushes, the koala has been seen eating only a few dozen, and seems to prefer just a handful. While the koala is occasionally found in other Australian trees, such as wattle, tea tree, or paperbark, scientists so far believe that koalas rely on the eucalyptus for food and cannot survive for very long on other trees.

The tough, smelly eucalyptus leaves contain oil and toxic chemicals that are potentially poisonous to most animals. The oil in eucalyptus leaves contains *cineole*, which can kill bacteria in the digestive tracts of most animals, leading to illness and even death. The koala's food habits and digestive system are designed to cope with strong toxicity of the eucalyptus leaves. Besides the koala, only the greater glider and ringtail possum are able to live on a diet of eucalyptus.

Not all eucalyptus trees are safe for the koala to eat. The koala's rubbery nose, covered in fine hairs, is an important tool used to ensure that it does not eat leaves that it cannot digest. The koala typically sniffs the tree trunks and leaves to determine if the tree species is palatable or too toxic. However, scientists are still unsure about what makes a particular tree appealing to a particular koala.

After making sure the leaves are edible, the koala uses its sharp claws to tear leaves from the branches of the eucalyptus, gathering as much as two pounds of leaves every day. The koala breaks off the leaves with its sharp incisor teeth, stacks the leaves in its big cheek pouches, then chews with its heavy blunt molars. The animal grinds the leaves until they become a fine pulp, which it then swallows.

Digestion

The koala consumes up to 2.5 pounds of eucalyptus leaves every day. But it has to work hard to digest the eucalyptus leaves, which contain very few nutrients. With a slow metabolic rate, the koala retains food in the digestive system long enough to extract enough nutrients to supply adequate energy.

Crucial to the digestive process is the caecum, a long tube where the food goes after being broken down in the small intestine. The caecum is common to herbivores, or animals that eat only plants. The koala's caecum is very long, about four times its body length. Microorganisms in the caecum help break down the carbohydrates in the leaf fiber, which are then absorbed into the bloodstream and carried to the liver, where they are converted into energy-providing glucose.

Certain eucalyptus leaves also contain prussic acid, a cyanide compound, that is most concentrated, and lethal, in new shoots of leaves. This substance is noxious even to koalas, so a koala has to be careful not to eat young shoots of certain species of eucalyptus.

While eucalyptus leaves are toxic, they do have a high water content. Koalas have a well-earned reputation for not drinking water; they are able to satisfy their thirst by eating the leaves. Thus, koalas, who are more vulnerable to cars, dogs, or other dangers on the ground are able to stay in the trees and avoid taking too many dangerous trips to seek out water sources. Koalas also get water from raindrops. If water is available in rivers or streams, the koala is able to drink directly. However, in times of drought, which are frequent in Australia, eucalyptus leaves dry up, as do streams, leaving the koala in danger of death from both thirst and starvation.

Koala colonies

A diet that is low in nutrition and high in toxic compounds leaves the koala with little energy left for activity. This contributes to the koala's overall lethargic lifestyle. The koala's brief daily activity usually does not include social behavior, except between mother and joey or adult males and females during breeding season. Only females and their young share trees with each other.

A male koala claims his territory by secreting a strong odor from a scent gland seen on the chest of this young male.

But koalas are not solitary animals. Scientists have found that koalas, while they feed individually in trees, actually live in small colonies, or social groupings made up of individuals with overlapping home ranges. A koala social group is centered around a dominant male, whose territory overlaps the territories of several females, joeys, and young adults who are still with their mothers. The number of koalas in a group varies according to the available food trees, but may range from three or four to ten or more. When the social structure is disturbed, such as when individual koalas are removed and relocated, or when a colony is disrupted by habitat loss, then the whole colony may collapse.

The male claims his territory by secreting a strong odor from the scent gland on his chest and leaving it on the base of a tree. This scent attracts females and warns other males who are not welcomed in his territory. The dominant male is active at night during breeding season, when he will move around his territory, pushing out male rivals and mating with receptive females. The dominant male will also lead the group to a new area of trees once the leaves of the local trees have been depleted.

Koalas use a variety of sounds to communicate with each other. Males have a deep grunting bellow used to proclaim their presence and dominance. They also bellow to express aggression and as part of their mating behavior. Mothers and joeys make soft clicking, squeaking, humming, and murmuring sounds to each other. They grunt to express displeasure and annoyance. When they are fearful or under extreme stress, koalas of both sexes let out a high-pitched cry.

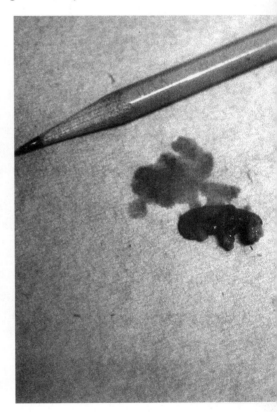

A joey weighs only about 0.5 grams at birth, and measures less than an inch in length.

Mating behavior

The calls are loudest when koalas are ready to mate. Both sexes use their vocal abilities to attract the opposite sex. "The male begins by calling out, making a deep, grunting sound, a bellow, which not only attracts females but also warns other males to stay away. A female who is ready for mating will answer back,"[4] writes Simon Hunter in *The Official Koala Handbook.*

Taking advantage of the warmer spring and summer months, the breeding season for koalas spans the year from September to March, although there are variations from the north to the south in the range. Koalas are born during the months of the year when tree foliage is freshest and most available.

Birth

While almost all marsupial females do not have a placenta to nourish their young in the womb, koalas have a basic placenta, but it is not sufficient to provide gestation for much longer than about one month. A koala pregnancy lasts just thirty-five days before the joey emerges, pink, hairless, and nearly transparent. It weighs only 0.5 grams, about as big as a bee. Healthy female koalas are able to give birth to one joey every year.

The koala is one of the few mammals who does not build or burrow a nest for its young. Rather, the koala, who is constantly moving from tree to tree in search of fresh foliage, gives birth on whatever eucalyptus branch it happens to be sitting on. The tiny newborn crawls through the mother's fur, seeking the nipple in her pouch. The pouch opens to the rear so that the joey can easily slip inside. Then the joey attaches itself to one of its mother's two nipples and begins to suck. The joey remains inside her closed pouch, firmly attached to the nipple in both waking and sleeping states, for at least five months.

At seven weeks, the joey's head is about twenty-six millimeters, even larger than its body. The eyes open when the joey is about twenty-two weeks old. At this time, it will poke its head out of the pouch for the first time. The joey is covered with fur and has its first teeth when it is twenty-four weeks old. At thirty weeks, the joey spends most of the time outside the pouch, though still clinging to the mother. The joey can emerge from the pouch and separate from its mother for brief periods of time when it is thirty-seven weeks old. Gradually, the joey is able to spend more time away from its mother, though it still drinks its mother's milk and spends much of the day on her back.

At twelve months, the joey weighs more than two kilograms and it is time for it to be weaned. During the weaning process, the joey eats the digested gum leaves which the mother has passed out of her body as excrement. This digested matter contains the bacteria that the young koala needs in order to develop its own digestive system and to begin breaking down the tough, noxious leaves in its own stomach.

Young koalas reach maturity when they are about two years old. Females are able to begin mating at this time. Males usually wait until they are about four years old and large enough to compete for females. The young males usually get chased away from their mothers during the breeding season. They spend a few years wandering, a time when they are especially at risk for ground dangers. When he is four or five years old, the male koala will claim his own territory and begin to mate. Some young females may also leave their mother's home territory in search of new forests and a dominant male, but most will stay in the same range all their lives.

Home range

The area of habitat needed by a koala depends on the abundance of food trees. A koala can live in a relatively small area if it has access to enough trees. Once the koala establishes a home range, it will stay in it for life, if food trees are sufficient. Even when its home range is destroyed by development, the koalas will remain in the area, looking for the trees that were once there. "We soon learned that koalas are so territorial that if a corridor [a band of vegetation which connects distinct patches of forest] is destroyed and a housing development put in its place, koalas—whose ancestors for hundreds of years may have passed along that land in search of trees—will continue to use the corridor, even falling into swimming pools,"[5] writes koala expert Ken Phillips.

Once the adult male settles on its home range, it maps out the boundaries by leaving his scent and scratch marks on tree trunks, and fecal pellets on the ground near the base of trees that his scent and it visits regularly all during its life. "Such trees are considered to be critical in maintaining social cohesion"[6] in a koala colony, according to Sharp, of the Australian Koala Foundation (AKF). If those critical trees are cut down or removed, the koala will become disoriented, even though there may be other trees available.

In adequate habitat, the koala will move from tree to tree, day by day, allowing the trees to regrow leaves. But if there are not enough food trees locally, the koala will have to wander outside its range for food. The size

A male koala maps out his home range by leaving scratch marks on the trees in the area.

of a home range varies widely from one to seven or more acres, depending on the availability of food trees.

Life expectancy

The fortunate koala, with plenty of edible eucalyptus woodland, can live a relatively long life of ten or more years. A few females and males followed by the Koala Preservation Society of New South Wales were found to live between thirteen and eighteen years. Males generally do not live as long as females. This is because male koalas travel more, putting them at risk for injury, accidents, and starvation. Also, males typically do not get the prime habitat or best food trees, which are taken by nursing females and joeys.

Stress and disease

Scientists have found that the koala is vulnerable to stress, particularly when there are changes in its environment or food supply. Because koalas do not store fat, when they do not have an adequate diet, their muscles quickly break down to convert into energy. Loss of habitat and food trees also causes stress in the koala.

Stress occurs when external factors cause an animal to become sick or even die. When stress levels increase, the koala becomes vulnerable to disease, a significant cause of death for koalas. The koala is susceptible to the bacterium *Chlamydia* (see sidebar), as well as leukemia and skin cancers. In addition, they tend to suffer from ulcers, dehydration, and muscle wasting.

Overcrowding in small habitats is a risk factor for disease, since koalas who are living in close proximity are more apt to spread contagious diseases. "As suitable habitat becomes fragmented [large continuous forest patches which have become small patches of forest surrounded by disturbed areas] and dwindles in size due to human activities, the diseases play a more important role in the surviving koala population. Crowding of koalas into remaining habitats must lead to increased transmission of infectious diseases, and an increase in physiological stresses due to intraspecific conflict and competition for food,"[7] states

Chlamydia

Koalas are susceptible to many diseases. The most common is *Chlamydia*, a bacterium that is linked with a variety of infections in koalas. These infections may occur in the koala's urinary, reproductive, and respiratory tracts, as well as in the animal's eyes.

Epidemics of eye disease in koalas have been recorded for over one hundred years. *Chlamydia* can cause conjunctivitis, an eye infection that can lead to blindness. *Chlamydial* infection can also cause reproductive tract disease, leading to infertility in females. The bacterium is linked to chest infections. In addition, *Chlamydia* appears in a urinary tract disease known as "wet bottom" or "dirty tail," referring to the wet fur on the animal's rump, an infection that can move to the bladder and the kidneys, eventually killing the animal.

Chlamydia is widespread among koalas in the wild. Spread through sexual activity and other direct contact with infected body parts, *Chlamydia* is highly contagious in a koala colony. Females can pass the infection to their young. Only a few island populations have remained free of the disease.

Chlamydia seems to be most potent and harmful to koala colonies that are under stress. It travels quickly through koala populations that are already weakened by lack of food or habitat and can wipe out colonies of koalas. However, some koalas do produce an immune response to *Chlamydia* and are able to continue to breed.

While *Chlamydia* is considered a serious threat for koalas, it has controlled the growth of koala populations that do not have adequate food trees and habitat. There is no cure for *Chlamydia*, but koalas in captivity can be treated with antibacterial drugs to reduce the symptoms.

Chlamydia is a common bacteria that can lead to blindness and other serious health problems in the koala.

Professor W. Robinson of the Department of Veterinary Pathology at the University of Queensland.

Few choices

Koalas do not cope well with many stressful situations. This may be because koalas have a relatively small brain compared to other mammals of the same size. Scientists believe its small brain may minimize the koala's capacity to engage in a variety of behaviors and adapt to change. "Compared to most other mammals koalas show a limited range of behaviors, and a limited capacity to vary from these or to learn new ones,"[8] write koala experts Roger Martin and Kathrine Handasyde in *The Koala: Natural History, Conservation and Management*. The koala's limited behaviors may reduce its ability to survive when its environment changes.

Yet this ancient marsupial has survived for millions of years with few defenses, using only the small portions of nutrients and water derived from eucalyptus leaves. Adequate food trees, a safe home territory, and a stable colony are the most important elements of a koala's life. But because the koala is so specialized in what it eats and where it lives, it is not able to withstand changed circumstances. The animal survives best when conditions for food, habitat, and social group are stable.

Today, the koala is less apt to find the calm, predictable surroundings it needs to stay healthy. Habitat destruction and conflicts with human activities have jeopardized the koala in many parts of its range. Loss of an important food tree may cause a koala to wander off its home range and onto a dangerous highway, or up a utility pole, where it will risk starvation. Without sufficient eucalyptus foliage, the koala has no alternative food source.

2

Vanishing Eucalyptus

THE EUCALYPTUS TREE is the koala's world. The joey slips out of its mother's womb in the branches of the tree. It grows and feeds on its leaves. After maturing, the young adult mates in the shadowy canopy of the trees. During the day, the koala sleeps in the eucalyptus tree's secure fork. At night, it may slip down the trunk, hurry across the ground, and quickly climb up a new tree.

The koala relies on eucalyptus trees for survival, so if these trees disappear, the koala will be threatened with extinction. Researchers worry that this scenario is already occurring in some places. Australia's eucalyptus woodlands are shrinking at an alarming rate. Some people estimate that 80 percent of the original eucalyptus forests in east and southeast Australia have already been destroyed, leaving the koala in many places with only patches and remnants of its historic habitat.

In the two centuries since the European settlement of Australia, eucalyptus forests have been eliminated by logging, grazing, farming, and urban and suburban development. Australia's dry climate and fragile, thin soils, coupled with poor land management, such as overgrazing and clear-felling forests, has increased the risk that the koala's woodlands will succumb to natural phenomena, such as drought and fire.

With few protections in place for existing koala habitat, the pressure on the koala's forests are likely to continue. Also, the majority of koalas live on privately owned land, which is generally not shielded against development or

The unique ecosystem of Australia features various species of eucalyptus trees.

other uses that conflict with koalas and other native wildlife. Thus, the human impact on the koala's historic range appears only to be increasing.

Australia's native tree

The eucalyptus forests and open woodlands of east and southeast Australia offer a unique ecosystem, providing habitat for the koala and hundreds of other animals and plants found nowhere else on earth. Most forests with eucalyptus trees contain a cluster of three or more species, as well as other types of trees and vegetation. These forests are known as sclerophyll forests, meaning the trees have hard-leaf foliage. In the sclerophyll forest, the individual koala favors and feeds on only a few species of eucalyptus trees, including Manna Gums, Swamp Gums, River Red Gums, and Blue Gums, each more prevalent in different parts of the country.

Like the koala, eucalyptus trees are native to Australia, although they have been planted in many countries with mild climates. The genus *Eucalyptus* includes over seven hundred species of trees and shrubs, ranging from dwarf ornamental shrubs to tall timber trees, all of which thrive in warm climates, poor soil, extreme heat, unreliable weather, and even drought. The word *eucalyptus* is a Greek word, meaning "well-covered," which refers to the buds that are covered with a cup-shaped membrane before bursting into flower.

Commonly known as gum trees or gums, because of the resin which drips from the cuts in their trunks, eucalyptus are hardwood trees that are evergreen. Loose bark peels from some of the tree trunks, a feature that can pose a fire hazard and threat for koalas. Koalas are able to rely on the eucalyptus foliage year round, since the trees do not lose their leaves seasonally, although the leaves do drop off throughout the year. Within their tough waxy coatings, the leaves conserve nutrients and retain water, a necessity for the koala, which ingests water from eucalyptus.

Eucalyptus forests radiate a soft gray-blue color, due to the thick waxy coating and oil content of the leaves. The oil discourages most animals from eating the leaves, though not the koala. The oil also gives off a distinctive medicinal smell, often associated with cough medicine.

Colonial clearing for settlements

The koala's habitat was not significantly disrupted during the time of the Aborigines. The indigenous Australians were the only human inhabitants of the continent from about fifty thousand years ago until 1788, when British colonists arrived. The Aborigines, who sparsely populated the island, were nomadic hunter-gatherers who cleared some forest undergrowth and used the hardwood of the eucalyptus trees for tools, weapons, housing, and fuel, but they left the forests mostly intact.

Prior to European settlement of Australia, forests and woods with eucalyptus trees stretched from the Queensland rain forests in the north to the coast of the Bass Strait

The native Aborigines left forest areas largely intact, posing no threat to koala habitat.

in southern Victoria and around the southeast corner of South Australia. Historians estimate that, at the time of European colonization, the eucalyptus woodlands in the four states with koalas covered about 762,600 square miles. Koalas, probably numbering in the millions, were scattered through much of this area, mostly in the warm coastal regions, rather than in higher altitudes inland.

Although the Aborigines hunted the koala for food and fur, and the native dog, the dingo, preyed on the animal, the koala population was stable at this time. But the Aborigines, and the eucalyptus forests, were in for a change. A fleet of eleven ships carrying about 750 convicts and 250 soldiers and colonial administrators sailed into Botany Bay near present-day Sydney on January 20, 1788. There they established the first European settlement in Australia, a penal colony for Great Britain. They hoped that their new country would prove profitable for farming and raising livestock. To make way for settlements, the colonists had to clear the trees.

The koala population temporarily increased after European settlement. Aborigines were displaced by settlers in the forests on the east coast, reducing the threat of the subsistence koala hunting. The dingos were chased away by settlers fearing for their livestock, stemming predation of the koala. During the early years of settlement, koalas were seen as far north as Cooktown in northern Queensland. The early British naturalist John Gould wrote in 1863 that he spotted koalas throughout the lush foliage along the eastern and southern coasts. This was a temporary reprieve for the koala. By the late nineteenth century, the settlers would discover the commercial value of the koala's pelt and the durability of the eucalyptus wood.

Its habitat soon came under siege. Eucalyptus trees began falling quickly, as the early settlers cut down the forests of eastern Australia to build houses, barns, and community buildings, and to open fields to raise food and livestock. "The new settlers brought with them axes and saws and, as they pushed further inland, usually along the watercourses, the sound of falling trees began to echo through the valleys,"[9] writes koala historian Bill Phillips.

Eucalyptus wood products

The settlers found eucalyptus wood to be useful for many purposes, from tools to housing. They used the wood of the River Red Gum, a tree that is favored by koalas and is durable and resistant to frost, heat, and drought, to build ships and houses, bridges and mine supports, railway sleepers, cabinets, crafts, and woodchips. Other gum trees were also found to be useful in construction.

The koala's favored trees contain an oil that became a valuable commercial product for the settlers. An industry in eucalyptus oil began in the 1850s and 1860s in Victoria and New South Wales. In addition, the trees contain tannins, a compound used to treat and strengthen leather. Soon, eucalyptus was being cut and shipped out for export to England's tanneries, or leather factories, leaving behind disturbed koala habitat and fewer standing food trees.

Settlers found the wood of the River Red Gum, favored by the koala, useful in building bridges and other structures.

Farming and grazing

Felling forests to make way for farms and large-scale agricultural production also removed available habitat from koalas. In some places, farms displaced koala populations entirely. The decline and near extinction of the koala population in the Bega Valley in the southeast corner of New South Wales was caused by the cutting down of the eucalyptus trees, which were almost completely eliminated when the forest was converted to farmland around 1905.

Early settlers found that Australia, with its thin soil and dry climate, was more suitable for grazing than it was for farming. More eucalyptus trees were cut down so that sheep and cattle could graze on open grasslands. The wool industry, now one of Australia's most important industries, grew rapidly in the early nineteenth century. Australia's eastern forests were cut down to make way for grazing land. By the time one hundred years had passed, some eight million cattle and one hundred million sheep were grazing on the fields. Today, Australia is the world's largest supplier of wool for clothing. The industry is centered in the east, much of it on grasslands carved from former hardwood forests.

Livestock provides an important source of income to many Australians, but it competes with koalas. Replacing forests with pasture land removes koala food trees. In addition, the grazing of sheep and cattle amidst the remaining open woodlands causes severe habitat degradation and interrupts the natural regeneration of native trees and plants. Grazing eliminates young seedlings, so that new trees aren't able to take root.

Clearing away native vegetation also contributes to streambed erosion, which in turn harms the roots of eucalyptus trees that grow near creeks, a favorite spot for koalas because scientists theorize the fertile soil seems to make the leaves more palatable. Thus, overgrazing can damage forest remnants that remain standing at the edge of fields and alongside rivers or streams, eventually damaging and even killing koala food trees.

Sandmining is another industry that has disturbed koala habitat. Mining for valuable hard metals in sandy soil is a lucrative industry in Australia, but one that has inflicted damage on natural areas, particularly in eastern woodlands and coastal areas. The mining process requires the removal of all surface vegetation, including trees. Koala advocates have long urged sandmining companies to avoid activity in areas with koalas.

Human settlement

Along with clearing land for grazing, agriculture, and mining, the settlers cut down trees so that they could build towns and cities. At first, the settlements hugged the east coast, where the climate was best and the land was most fertile. This region has more rainfall than other parts of Australia, making it better for farming and grazing. It was also the core of the koala's range.

The gold rush in Victoria and New South Wales in the 1850s brought thousands of new settlers from the coastal regions to the inland areas of southeast Australia, and they

The human settlements during the 1850 gold rush in Victoria and New South Wales disrupted the low-lying fertile koala habitat.

cleared land and chopped down trees to build farms and homes. The settlers found that the low-lying fertile open woodlands near rivers were the best places to plant crops, graze cattle, and build homes. Since koalas favor trees near water sources, this was harmful to their population. "These areas also supported the most productive eucalyptus forests and, from our present knowledge of the dietary and habitat preferences of koalas, would have contained the most abundant populations,"[10] write koala experts Martin and Handasyde. Thus, the clearing of these fertile land was extremely detrimental to koalas.

Today, the east coast of Australia is the most populous part of the country, leaving little room for native wildlife. "Australia's three largest urban centers, Melbourne, Sydney and Brisbane, are founded on what were once prime koala habitats,"[11] writes koala historian Bill Phillips. As the cities continue to expand in the surrounding suburbs, koalas in many places are increasingly under pressure from conflicts with human activities.

Koalas in Queensland

In Queensland, on Australia's northeast coast, the koala is listed as "common wildlife" under the Nature Conservation (Wildlife) Regulation of 1994. Queensland has the largest population of koalas in Australia, estimated at twenty-five thousand to fifty thousand by the Australian Koala Foundation (AKF) in the mid-1990s. Thus, koalas are not considered endangered in Queensland, one of the most rapidly urbanizing regions of Australia, but the animal is slowly declining due to the clearing of forests and woodlands, development, and agriculture.

In Queensland, as in other parts of Australia, koalas live primarily on forested farms and other private property. Because the koala is not considered endangered, private landowners are not required to protect koalas or other animals on their property. Rather, the animal's survival depends on landowners voluntarily protecting habitat. In the semiarid woodlands of central and southwest Queensland, over one million acres are being cleared annually for crops and grazing fields.

Flagship Species

The koala's role as an Australian mascot has improved its chances for survival because many people are exposed to the animal and concerned for its welfare. Its familiar image is a source of inspiration for both popular culture and conservation. Sympathetic koala characters appear in aboriginal legends, children's books, and advertising for food, medicine, and the travel industry in Australia. A study by the Australia Institute showed that $1.1 billion (Australian dollars) was brought into the Australian economy in 1996 by foreign tourists who came to see koalas.

Because it is one of the more popular mammals in the world, the koala is considered a flagship species. A flagship species is a well-known animal that holds the "flag" for its habitat. Protecting a flagship species guarantees protection to other species in the same habitat. "They are powerful icons for conservation," write Elaine Stratford and coauthors in *Conservation Biology* in describing the koala.

Thus, saving a eucalyptus forest for koalas also preserves the habitat of the Nephila spider, which lays eggs on the branches of River Red Gums. The emperor gum moth constructs cocoons on the branches of the eucalyptus trees. Sugar gliders, a marsupial, virtually fly among the treetops on flaps of skin that link their limbs. Powerful owls swoop into the forest to snatch opossums, and occasionally young koalas, for food. On the ground, the short-beaked echidna, a monotreme, forages for termite and ant nests. In the grasses, snakes glide and an eastern water dragon crawls among the litter of leaves and fallen bark. The scaly-breasted lorikeets build nests in the tree hollows, while finches flit through the bushes and vegetation.

When a eucalyptus forest comes under threat, the potential loss of a spider or a moth might not arouse much public concern. But threats to the koala draw widespread attention to the fragileness of the forest ecosystem and the need to protect its biodiversity. Consequently, efforts to save the koala's woodlands have a ripple effect, improving the chances that lesser-known species that share its trees, whose extinction might otherwise have gone unnoticed, will survive as well.

Unique and lovable icons, koalas gain protection for its habitat as a flagship species.

The koalas living in and around Brisbane, the state capital located in southeastern Queensland, are especially at risk for habitat loss. Clearing land to make way for urban expansion for the growing city and its surrounding suburbs has threatened one of the largest koala populations in Queensland. Suburban sprawl covers much of the historic koala habitat, except areas preserved in parks and wildlife refuges.

Hazards of civilization

A koala stranded at the top of a telephone or utility pole is a familiar sight in many Australian suburbs, where koala populations survive in remnant woodlands on the outskirts of cities. The koala's natural instinct is to climb tree trunks. When it is unable to find a eucalyptus tree, the koala will climb a wood pole, such as a telephone pole, only to discover that there are no leaves to eat. It will then move on and continue its search for leaves, but it will already be weakened by hunger and stress.

Mistaking utility poles for food trees is one of many hazards facing koalas in developed regions. The expansion of urban and suburban communities into koala habitat creates serious problems for the wild animal. Swimming pools and backyard fences are deadly traps for koalas. It is not uncommon for koalas walking in search of a eucalyptus tree to stumble into a suburban swimming pool, then be unable to climb out. Even a backyard fence can create a problem for a confused koala. It may have the ability to climb over it, but is too disoriented to escape.

Koalas are also frequently attacked by domestic dogs. Unrestrained dogs are considered a major cause of koala deaths in regions where historic habitat has turned into suburbs. Between 1995 and 1997, 356 koalas suffering from dog attacks were admitted to the Queensland Parks and Wildlife Services' Moggill Hospital, a koala hospital.

The AKF estimates that about four thousand koalas are killed each year by dogs and motor vehicles. Vehicular traffic poses risks for koalas, particularly in areas where highways and roads cut through koala habitat. The koala's gray and brown fur may provide camouflage in the eucalyptus trees, but the subdued colors prevent drivers from spotting the animal on the road before it is too late. Since koalas are nocturnal and tend to move on the ground only at night, drivers are particularly at risk of hitting one. Koalas are especially prone to injury and attacks during breeding season, from September to March, when they are likely to move more frequently on the ground in search of mates.

In Port Macquarie, a fast-growing resort area on the coast of New South Wales, it is not uncommon to find an injured koala limping along the side of the road, hit by a car. This region was formerly a eucalyptus forest; now it is a busy community. Along Highway 31, north of Melbourne, Victoria, road signs warn of koalas crossing, yet dead koalas are frequently seen on the side of the road. In the Redlands region of Queensland, near Brisbane, home to thousands of koalas, some 350 are killed each year by cars and hundreds more are injured or orphaned.

Commercial logging

While early settlers cut down eucalyptus trees to build their own homes, boats, and tools, a commercial lumber industry was gradually established, reliant, in part, on the sclerophyll forests in eastern Australia. This industry would prove perilous to koalas and other forest wildlife. Intensive lumbering often meant clear-cutting, or removing all the trees, in large areas of forest, leaving little chance for natural regrowth.

Road signs in Australia alert travelers of koala crossings.

Beginning in the 1930s, the Australian states established public forests, protected from private ownership and development, but open to the timber industry. Timber companies lease tracts of land in the forests, then harvest the wood for use in a variety of products. Until recently, there were few protections in the state forests for wildlife or native plants.

In Australia, as in other countries, there are conflicting values when it comes to managing the public forests. The states try to conserve plants and animals, protect water, and offer recreational and educational opportunities, as well as provide timber and other forest products. In this way, the states try to balance the values of conservation and economic growth.

Yet conservationists have criticized Australian states for managing the public forests for industry, rather than for wildlife and native flora protection. For example, a significant koala population, ranging from several thousand to over ten thousand, inhabits the Pilliga forests, an area of woodlands and forests encompassing about two million acres located on the northwest slopes and plains of New South Wales. Most of the woodlands are in state forests and nature reserves, but less than 10 percent of the area is protected for nature conservation. Logging has imperiled the koalas and the wide diversity of other animals in the state forests.

Though potentially damaging to the environment, logging is an important part of Australia's economy. The estimated sixty thousand people who work in the $6 billion forest-products industry need their jobs. "Jobs mean survival for little towns like Orbost [in Victoria]. Without logging people move out. There's just no other industry here,"[12] said one logger who was cutting trees in a forest in East Gippsland, Victoria. The logger was leaning against an ancient eucalyptus tree that had just been felled. The logger was cutting mostly old-growth trees, because those are most profitable. Timber companies value old-growth wood because it is strong, large in diameter, with a fine grain, and yields a higher profit than wood from younger trees.

Wood chipping

Most recently, forest clearing for the wood chip industry has come under scrutiny for its harmful effect on the koala and other native Australian wildlife. Over half the wood logged in Australia's native forests, including eucalyptus woodlands, is made into wood chips for export and processing into paper products. Ancient trees are felled, then ground

up to make computer printing paper, tissue, and other products. Japanese paper and paper products companies are a major consumer of Australia's wood chips.

Over six million tons of wood chips are exported from Australia's forests to companies in Japan each year, according to The Wilderness Society, an Australian environmental organization. "Australian conservation groups contend that their country's forest heritage is being systematically ground up into wood chips and loaded onto ships, mostly bound for Japan,"[13] writes Mark Clayton of the *Christian Science Monitor*. There are limits on wood chip exports, but environmentalists would like even more restrictions, especially in ancient forests, where habitat for native wildlife is being chopped up and lost forever.

A group of protesters in Sydney, Australia, dressed in koala suits oppose the clearing of koala habitat for the wood chip industry.

Bush fire

Human activities have harmed the koala's habitat indirectly as well. Bush fire, or forest fire, is a natural phenomenon in Australia that has been exacerbated by human activities, leading to increased threats to the koala. Prior to colonization, the Aborigines kept the forest floors clear of debris through their practice of firestick farming and regular burning to enable grasses to grow. But the settlers did not practice forest management. Fallen bark and leaves were allowed to accumulate, so that when fire occurred, it was particularly devastating. Also, the felling of Australia's native forests for industry and development left patches of woodlands separated by treeless land. Fragmented forests are more vulnerable to fire because they are framed by flammable brush rather than protected by other forests. Thus, bush fires have increased since the European settlement of Australia.

Bush fires are deadly in a eucalyptus forest, since the trees shed their bark, branches, and leaves and deposit a thick layer of tinder on the forest floor. Crown fires, when flames roar through the tree-tops of eucalyptus forests, move rapidly and, often, uncontrollably.

A fire sweeping through a eucalyptus woodland is particularly lethal to the slow-moving koala. The gum trees virtually explode because of the toxic oil in the leaves, and not much is left behind. Koalas cannot move quickly

A fire sweeps across a forest of eucalyptus trees in Tasmania, Australia, endangering the slow-moving koalas living there.

enough to escape the flames, so they are trapped in burning trees. "Koalas cannot escape bushfires; even if they are not killed outright, they suffer burns when descending to the ground to change trees, debilitation and dehydration . . . and difficulty breathing from smoke inhalation,"[14] writes koala expert Ann Sharp.

Many local extinctions of koalas during the last two hundred years are blamed on bush fires. "Koalas are highly vulnerable to fires that burn the forest canopy, and when such fires occur koalas are eliminated over considerable areas,"[15] write Martin and Handasyde. A major fire in Victoria in 1851 inflicted large-scale damage on woodlands. Bush fires are the reason for "the generally low number of koalas thought to be surviving in Victoria in the early 1900s,"[16] they note.

Koalas lose food trees

Fires continue to threaten Australia's koalas. In September 1994, brush fires swept through woodlands near Port Stephens and Port Macquarie in New South Wales, wiping out significant koala habitat. The fires, the result of a long drought, spelled disaster for koalas. Then in 1997, a bush fire destroyed much of the Pilliga nature reserve near the township of Connabarabran in New South Wales, another important koala habitat. Hundreds of koalas were believed to have been killed by the fire, which brought out more than six thousand firefighters. The fire was considered an environmental catastrophe for the forest's rare and endangered species, including other marsupials, such as the brush-tailed rock wallaby and the Pilliga mouse. Eighty percent of the nature reserve was destroyed. Hundreds of koalas lost their trees.

Once a woodland has burned, koalas cannot return to it for many years. Eucalyptus trees are somewhat adapted to fire, for some species need extreme heat to burst open their button-shaped pods and release their seeds. Thus, after a bush fire, it is possible for seeds to successfully germinate. Also, some eucalyptus can regenerate from buds beneath the bark or from lignotubers, root-like structures beneath

A volunteer cares for a koala injured in a massive, devastating, woodland fire.

the ground. But it takes many years for a eucalyptus tree to grow tall enough to support koalas.

Drought, another natural phenomenon in Australia that is disastrous to koalas, has also been on the increase, in part because of human activities. Drought worsens with overuse of natural resources, such as draining fields or diverting waterways, and poor land management. Managing land poorly ranges from overgrazing to failing crop-rotation standards. Drought can weaken and damage eucalyptus trees, leaving the koala without food and water resources. In addition, drought contributes to fire. In October 2000, a severe drought in Southeast Queensland contributed to fires that burned thousands of acres of forest and farmland, a disaster for koalas, possums, and other animals living in the trees.

Habitat degradation

Along with increased occurrence of drought and bush fire, Australia has struggled with environmental problems resulting from poor land management and fragmented forests. These contribute to worse conditions for koalas. Overuse of land for crops and grazing, and clear-cutting in forests, have caused natural areas to degrade and become vulnerable to problems such as erosion, insect infestation, and an Australian phenomenon known as dieback, a general term for the gradual dying of trees, all of which directly harm koalas. Small isolated areas of forests are especially prone to dieback. The trees die for many reasons, from soil erosion and general land degradation to rising water levels underground that creates salination, or salt in the soil.

By 1980, there was an epidemic of dieback in the farming regions inland from Sydney, posing a severe economic and ecological threat to local communities and wildlife, including the koala. Scientists found that a common beetle was causing this complex condition. The introduction of nonnative grasses and livestock create a fertile climate for beetles. Trees weakened by drought and soil erosion are unable to withstand an onslaught of insects. Koalas lost eucalyptus food trees as a result of the infestation and related problems.

Forest clearing continues to affect koalas

Land clearing remains the biggest threat to Australia's wildlife biodiversity, causing numerous extinctions and threats to many animals, including the koala. Much of Australia's original expanse of eastern woodlands is gone now, forcing the koala into small isolated fragments and patches of habitat, surrounded by human activity. Approximately 80 percent of the original eucalyptus forests are now gone, estimates the AKF.

In recent years, Australia has had one of the world's highest rates of forest clearance, ranking just after Brazil, Indonesia, the Congo, and Bolivia. Some 1.3 million acres were cleared in 1999, reported the Australian Conservation Foundation, the country's largest environmental group. In New South Wales, for example, about 379,500 acres of forest are cleared every year. In some parts of the state, more than 90 percent of all native vegetation has been lost, according to the New South Wales National Parks &

Koala's Favorite Trees

Part of the challenge of retaining habitat for koalas, and identifying new habitat where a koala colony could be established, is that the animals are fussy about what type of eucalyptus trees they feed on. During a survey of koalas by the Australian government in the mid-1980s, researchers sighted the koala in 120 different eucalyptus trees and 13 non-eucalyptus trees.

Scientists are beginning to gather more clues as to why an individual koala likes one tree and not another. Researchers from the Australian National University have found that the preference is related to the levels of formyl phloroglucinol compounds, or FPCs, that occur in eucalyptus leaves. These FPCs protect the trees from predators, and they are toxic and deter animals from eating the leaves. The more FPCs a tree contains, the less likely a koala will eat it because of the leaves' toxicity. Levels of FPCs vary among different species of eucalyptus, and also between different trees of the same species.

Researchers have developed a way of measuring FPC concentration in a eucalyptus tree. They are now planning to put radio collars with microphones on koalas on Phillip Island, Victoria. The koalas will be followed and their chewing will be carefully noted. Scientists will be able to find out which trees the koalas feed on. They will then observe which leaves the koalas are feeding on, and also determine the level of FPC in the foliage. This is an important step toward accurately predicting whether koalas will be able to survive in a particular forest.

Two koalas nestle among the leaves of a eucalyptus tree.

Wildlife Service. As more trees are cleared, less habitat remains for wildlife.

Fragmented range

The range and distribution of a species, or the geographic area over which it is found, is a good indicator of how well the animal is faring. The most critical threat to koalas is the fact that their remaining range, though still broad, is broken and fragmented. Much of the eucalyptus habitat is scattered in patches or remnants, small fragments or islands surrounded by cleared land. These areas are often not large enough to support the koalas that lived there before clearing. "At best, a checkerboard of habitats results, but too often vast swatches of rapidly eroding country have been created,"[17] write Anna Povey and Lindsay Brown in *Watching Wildlife: Australia*.

When habitat is broken into small pieces, koalas can become estranged from their colonies. Young males may have trouble establishing new ranges as it becomes dangerous to travel across the large cleared areas or roads and highways that separate patches of forest. Since koalas need social structure to survive, when colonies are disrupted, the koalas become stressed and more prone to illness. Australians are discovering that koalas confined to small, isolated home ranges face serious problems, which are typically difficult to resolve.

3

Islands and Overpopulation

WHILE LOSS OF forest habitat puts the koala's future in jeopardy, another threat to the animal occurs when populations live in the small, isolated patches of habitat that remain after roads cut through forest or woods are cleared for pastures. When koalas are restricted to limited areas, without opportunities for young koalas to move on and establish new home ranges, they often reproduce in such high numbers that their survival is imperiled.

Overcrowding has often resulted from well-intentioned efforts to relocate koalas to islands and other regions, where people assumed the animals would be safe from harm. After a few years, the koalas reproduced to such numbers that they do not have enough food trees. Overpopulation poses a serious threat both to the environment and to the animals. It can cause the koala to succumb to stress and disease, starvation, and inbreeding, which will weaken the koala species. At the same time, overgrazing has sometimes caused eucalyptus woodlands to die, causing serious environmental problems not limited to koalas.

Preventing koalas from overpopulating their home ranges and defoliating the eucalyptus trees has become a major concern for Australia. Overpopulation problems have also made people look at koalas differently—not just as a favorite native animal, but as a pest and potential threat to the environment. Solving the overpopulation problem is considered essential to ensuring the koala's well-being and long-term survival in the wild.

Population explosions

The overpopulation of limited habitats is an oft-occurring problem for koalas. Scientists believe that koalas do not have built-in physiological or behavioral controls to restrict population growth to the available food supply.

Ironically, the absence of disease in a colony can worsen a tendency for koalas to overpopulate their habitat. Koala populations that are free of diseases caused by *Chlamydia* can double their numbers every two or three years. While *Chlamydia* is considered a serious problem for some koala colonies, it has helped to keep some populations from growing too large for their habitats. Koala females with *Chlamydia* have a lower fertility rate than healthy koalas, so that their colonies will reproduce more slowly, if at all. Also, in infected populations, weaker animals seem to succumb to the disease, become sick, infertile, or die, while the stronger animals continue to reproduce.

When isolated populations do not carry the *Chlamydia* bacteria, such as koalas on French Island in Victoria and Kangaroo Island in South Australia, they tend to overpopulate their habitat. Phillip Island koalas, in Victoria, in contrast, have a high incidence of chlamydial infection, which has kept fertility rates down.

A female koala munches on the sparse leaves of a eucalyptus tree with her joey in her pouch.

Framlingham Bush

Framlingham Bush is an isolated remnant of native forest located in western Victoria. Eucalyptus food trees border the Hopkins River there. In 1970, thirty-seven koalas were moved to the forest from Victoria's French Island, which was becoming too crowded. But the koalas multiplied.

By the 1990s, the koala population had become so large it was defoliating and killing the trees. "As a result of the food shortage, the population crashed with thousands of koalas starving to death,"[18] write Martin and Handasyde. Some four thousand koalas died of starvation between 1996 and 1998, according to the Koala Rescue Foundation, an organization that focuses on saving koalas in crowded habitats. About one thousand koalas were relocated throughout Victoria to save them from starvation.

As in Framlingham Bush, koala overpopulation has often inadvertently resulted from the efforts of people to provide safe refuge for the animal. This occurred in several locations, particularly on islands where koala populations were established during the early 1900s at the height of the koala hunt. At this time, many people were concerned that the koala hunt would wipe out the species entirely. To save koalas, people began relocating the animals to islands with protected habitat, such as nature refuges, where they would be able to live without the threat of being hunted. Yet many of the islands did not have adequate space or enough eucalyptus trees to maintain koala populations as they reproduced over the course of many decades.

Kangaroo Island

One of these island destinations was Kangaroo Island, a large island off the coast of South Australia. Koalas did not occur there naturally, but there were plenty of eucalyptus trees on the island in 1923, when conservationists first brought koalas to the island from French Island in Victoria, where they were already overgrazing the trees.

At the time, koalas were in danger of extinction because of hunting in South Australia, the state located in the southeast corner of the continent. Conservationists expected that the species could begin to revive on a safe, protected island. Platypuses, brush turkeys, and wombats were introduced to this island for similar reasons. The conservationists released the koalas at Flinders Chase National Park, still a popular tourist destination for wildlife enthusiasts. The park had plentiful eucalyptus habitat.

In the next decades, koala colonies were established in parts of the island outside the national park as well. At the same time, however, much of the island's land outside parks was cleared for agriculture, reducing the eucalyptus habitat to only protected land for the koalas. Even as their food trees were reduced, the koala population grew rapidly. There were no natural population controls for the island's koalas. No wild predators posed a danger for the koalas and the population was free of *Chlamydia*. By the late 1990s, the koala population had soared to somewhere between five thousand and ten thousand. They spread across most of the island, living in the river valleys with eucalyptus food trees. The trees were dying from overbrowsing, and koalas were facing food shortages.

The Australian government feared the trees would die, while the koalas would face increasing food shortages. "The ecosystem is under threat, not just for koalas but for everything else. More trees will die, koalas will start starving and eventually they'll die—and they'll die a long, slow prolonged death,"[19] said Hugh Possingham of the Koala Management Task Force.

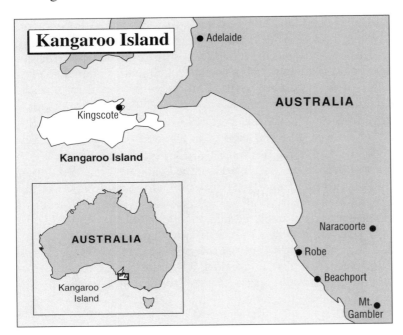

Koala Hunt

The koala's soft, durable fur drew hunters and traders to Australia's eucalyptus forests in the first decades of the twentieth century. The lethargic and defenseless koala, perched in a tree, was an easy target; the luxuriant koala pelt was just as easy to sell. In 1908, nearly sixty thousand koala pelts were sold in the Sydney marketplace. By 1919, a million or more koala skins were sold in Queensland. One million koalas were killed in New South Wales in 1924, a year when some 2 million koala skins were exported from Australia. Many skins were shipped to St. Louis, Missouri, which was a center for the fur trade.

The koala, at the time, was protected by law in parts of Australia. But because hunters formed a powerful political lobby, the government did not respond to the slaughter. As a result of the massacre, koalas were nearly extinct in South Australia by the mid-1920s, with koalas severely depleted in the states of New South Wales and Victoria. But Australian hunters did not stop searching out koalas in the eucalyptus forests, for they knew the animals were an easy mark. Along with guns, they used snares and cyanide poisoning, which left pelts unmarked.

Bowing to the political pressures of hunters to continue the koala hunt, in August 1927, Queensland, which had protected koalas since 1906 and so had one of the last remaining populations of koalas, declared an open season on koala hunting for thirty days and issued about ten thousand hunting licenses. In just one month, nearly six hundred thousand koalas were killed.

News of the Queensland hunt horrified the Australian people. As quoted in *Grzimek's Encyclopedia of Mammals*, the Australian zoologist Ellis Troughton had this to say about the hunt: "It is simply unbelievable that a civilized people could slaughter such a harmless indigenous animal solely for selfish gain." The Wildlife Preservation Society of Australia was formed in the late 1920s to protect the koala. In November 1927, the Commonwealth government banned the export of koala pelts. Soon after, U.S. president Herbert Hoover, who had worked in the gold fields of Australia, banned the importation of koala fur in the United States.

The damage had been done. By the 1930s, the koala was considered extinct in South Australia and nearly extinct in Victoria and New South Wales, while the animal steeply declined in Queensland. In 1934, an official in Victoria's government predicted that "on the mainland of Victoria, I feel certain, the koala is doomed to early extinction, and will never be reestablished, excepting perhaps in some reserves which may be specially set apart for its protection and conservation," writes koala expert Bill Phillips. It would take decades for the koala population to rebound. In some regions, the koala never returned.

Translocation in Victoria

Australia has tried a variety of techniques to cope with the problem of koala overpopulation. Translocation, or moving koalas from one place to another to relieve overcrowding, has been used for over a century. Victoria, the state located in the southeast corner of Australia, has had a long history of moving its koala populations—with a mixture of success.

Koala management through translocation in Victoria began in the 1920s as a response to the sharp decline in the mainland koala population in the early twentieth century. A combination of land clearing, hunting, disease, and large bush fires nearly wiped out the koala population in the state. By 1925, just five hundred koalas were left in Victoria and the species was heading for extinction. The aim of the program was to establish new koala colonies in areas that would not be prone to fire or human interference.

At the same time, French Island, in Western Port Bay, Victoria, was experiencing an overabundance of koalas.

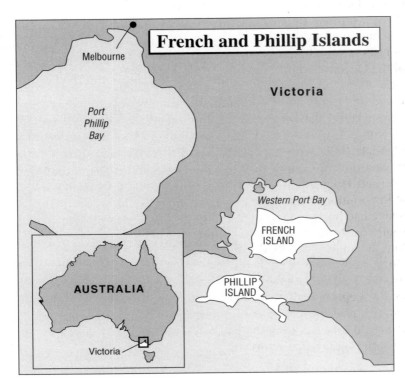

Koalas are not native to French Island. In 1898, a young farmer had released several koalas into the wild on the island. The koala population grew so rapidly that, by the early 1920s, a farmer counted twenty-three hundred koalas in one part of the island.

To relieve the overcrowding on French Island, and to establish koalas in other parts of the state, wildlife officials in 1923 captured and shipped fifty koalas to nearby Phillip Island. Other koalas were sent to Kangaroo Island, introducing the species to that island. Subsequently, every year, koalas were captured on French Island and relocated to islands and mainland Victoria. Thus, the island koalas escaped starvation, while new koala colonies were established in other locations.

Problems of overcrowding

Unfortunately, the introduced koala populations on Phillip Island and Kangaroo Island eventually erupted out of control. In the 1940s, more than three thousand koalas were removed from Phillip Island because of overcrowding. But by that time, the prime koala habitat had diminished and the koalas on Phillip Island were infected with *Chlamydia*, which reduced their fertility. Today, the Phillip Island koalas have fallen to such low numbers that efforts are underway to protect them.

Still, the koalas from French and Phillip Islands were used as a resource to restock the koala's historic range in Victoria. Over the years, wildlife officials translocated koalas from the islands to unoccupied habitat or areas with small koala colonies. Between 1923 and 1998, Victorian wildlife officials moved over 14,600 koalas.

Overall, translocation of koalas has been successful in Victoria. The process has enabled the koala to rebound from near-extinction in the early 1900s. Koalas have been reestablished in many parts of their former range. Today, the koala is distributed over much of lowland southern and eastern Victoria, and populations are high in many areas, according to the state government. However, much of the remaining habitat is fragmented, so populations are increasingly isolated and at risk for conflicts with human activity.

The challenges of translocation

Translocation is a complicated process, requiring a tremendous amount of funding, planning, and workers to make it successful. Each koala moved costs between $100 and $200 (Australian dollars), according to Martin and Handasyde. Koalas cannot be randomly moved without careful consideration of the individual animal's characteristics and the population it will join in the new location. For example, koala experts would not place a Northern koala in a population of Southern koalas because the two subspecies should remain distinct. Nor should koalas that carry *Chlamydia* be placed in a disease-free colony.

Adjusting to a new environment is not easy for any wild animal, particularly koalas, who react poorly to stress. In many ways, the moving process is just as difficult for the animals as adjusting to their new home. In October 2000, wildlife officers from the Victoria Department of Natural Resources and Environment transported some 250 koalas from French Island to mainland Victoria's Bunyip State

Tagged and ready for translocation, a koala peers out from his carrying case.

Catching a Koala

The process of sterilizing and translocating koalas to relieve overpopulation starts with the challenge of luring the animals down from the branches of the eucalyptus tree. Some koalas are wedged into tree branches as high up as sixty feet, and they generally do not come down voluntarily.

On Kangaroo Island, koala rescuers with a government-funded organization called Koala Rescue developed an effective routine in the late 1990s when they participated in efforts to slow down the local population explosion. Once a koala is spotted, a trained volunteer with professional climbing equipment ascends the tree, while carrying a metal pole with a loop of rope and a plastic flag. The rescuer throws a lasso over the koala, then waves the flag above its head to scare it into climbing down the tree. "Look, it's not easy. That's for sure. They're wild animals and don't take kindly to being captured out of their trees," said Drew Laslett, project manager of Koala Rescue, in *Time for Kids*.

When the koala reaches the ground, other volunteers help get it into a burlap sack. The volunteers have to be careful not to get scratched or bitten by an indignant koala, though once in a while, it happens. While *New York Times* reporter Clyde Farnsworth watched the process in April 1997, one teenage volunteer was bitten on the thigh as he tried to tag a koala's ear. But the teenager brushed off the potentially serious injury as "only a pinch."

The koala is then taken to a mobile surgical unit where it is sedated for surgery. A veterinarian is on hand to perform a vasectomy on males and a tubal ligation on females. The operations take only about fifteen minutes. After sterilization the koalas are returned to the same tree from which they were captured or relocated to another habitat. A microchip with a bar code is imbedded in each koala's shoulder so that they can be tracked in the future.

A worker from Koala Rescue coaxes a koala from a tree.

A koala is released for resettlement into a new habitat by a'rescue worker.

Park, near Gembrook. The koalas were first sterilized, then put into cages, two by two, transported by boat and then by truck to their new home. Two males ripped the bars from their cage. A couple of others escaped entirely. In another translocation project from Snake Island, Victoria, officials estimated that 12 percent of the koalas died of stress-related problems, such as unwillingness to feed in the new habitat.

Another challenge is finding the appropriate new habitat for the koalas. Individual koalas prefer certain types of eucalyptus trees; they may have difficulty adjusting to unfamiliar tree species. Sometimes koalas have been moved to sites that did not have an adequate supply of food trees. This happened on Quail Island, Victoria. French Island koalas were translocated to nearby Quail Island in the 1930s, but within a decade, hundreds of koalas on Quail Island were starving because they had overbrowsed the trees. Once again, koalas were caught and moved to other parts of Victoria.

Finally, translocation is not a permanent solution. Even after decades of moving koalas off French Island, koalas are still overcrowding the island. Habitat loss and fragmentation for koalas continue to be problems in Victoria, as in all of Australia. Finding appropriate habitat may become increasingly difficult. If there is not sufficient eucalyptus habitat available to relocate koalas, translocation will no longer be an option in Victoria. With available habitat running out on the mainland, alternatives to translocation are desperately needed.

Culling koalas

One option for controlling koala populations is to cull some of the animals, or selectively kill them, in order to reduce the numbers to a sustainable level. The idea was suggested in the 1990s on Kangaroo Island when the koala overpopulation was not only threatening the animals with starvation, but also inflicting ecological harm on the land. Some people felt the quickest, easiest, and least expensive way to deal with the problem was to kill some of the koalas, a method already used for kangaroos and wallabies on Kangaroo Island. Proponents of culling argued that it was more humane to shoot a koala than to watch it slowly die of starvation.

But because the koala is a very popular native animal in Australia, the idea was met with public opposition and dismay. "This is outrageous and a national disgrace. Koalas are a national icon,"[20] said Pam Allan, then New South Wales environment minister, in response to the proposal to kill koalas. The idea was put aside, though some people still feel that culling koalas is the best way to deal with the overpopulation problem.

Fertility control

A less controversial way to control koala populations is to reduce the birthrate so that the animals do not reproduce too rapidly. This can be done by using fertility controls on individual koalas. One advantage of fertility control is that it can be done on site, without requiring the koalas to be moved to other areas. Some fertility programs are reversible or temporary. They are also cost effective.

For isolated populations of up to several thousand animals, fertility control by hormone implants for females and vasectomies for males is feasible. Vasectomy of male koalas is a simple and safe operation. The surgery alters the male's reproductive organs so that it cannot impregnate females.

In the late 1990s, the Tower Hill State Game Reserve in southwestern Victoria was used as a study site for a fertility project. About 375 koalas lived in the reserve. Two hormones were applied to female koalas during June and July 1997. The hormones were administered in slow-release silicon tubes implanted under the koala's skin, a technique that is considered quick, safe, and effective. The fertility suppression can be reversed by removing the implants. A low dose of hormones was used to avoid any side effects or harm to the koalas. Vasectomies were performed on male koalas. A year later, scientists found a significantly lower birthrate in the colony. Nearly 100 percent of the animals will not reproduce.

Kangaroo Island rescue project

A combination of tactics is being used to manage the koala population on Kangaroo Island. In 1997, the government of South Australia launched the Koala Rescue project, which uses a combination of translocation, fertility control, and habitat restoration. Koalas were first sterilized, then relocated beginning in December 1997. Only sterilized koalas were relocated to ensure that overcrowding did not occur in the new habitat. By the summer of 2000, thirty-four hundred animals had been spayed or neutered, and eleven-hundred of the sterilized animals were moved off the island to woodlands on the mainland of South Australia. "We've probably slowed the growth rate. But we haven't stopped it,"[21] said Bob Inns, who supervises the program for South Australia's Department of Environment and Heritage.

The project also provides funds to preserve and restore eucalyptus woodlands on the island, many of which have already been severely overbrowsed. By protecting the habitat that remains, and planting trees to

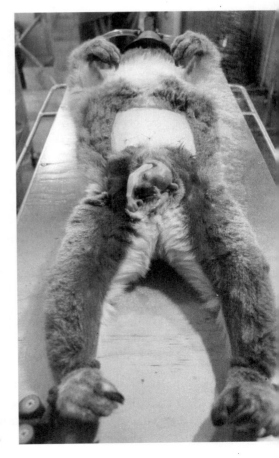

This female koala, with a joey in her pouch, is in the process of being sterilized as part of a program to protect the koala by limiting its population.

revegetate and expand the area available to koalas, the project will enable koalas to live on the island in the future. Access to adequate habitat will help to ensure that the koalas do not overbrowse the trees.

Not everyone favors the rescue project. Some critics say it is too expensive and time-consuming to be used in other locations as a solution for koala overcrowding. The Australian Koala Foundation (AKF) has criticized the project for removing koalas from their home colonies and disrupting their social structure. "If you take the leaders out of a family, you just get juvenile delinquency among the young males,"[22] said AKF executive director Deborah Tabart. The young males may mate too freely, causing a further population explosion, she said. Tabart favors more habitat preservation and restoration.

 ## Mount Eccles National Park

Safe from development or habitat loss, koalas in Mount Eccles National Park in Victoria have been able to thrive. Located on Victoria's southwest coast, the park encompasses an extinct volcano overlooking craters now filled with the waters of Lake Surprise. The land is covered with green heath and Manna Gum forest. Unfortunately, the koala population is also overbrowsing the leaves of the park's trees.

Koalas were first released at Mount Eccles in 1973, and also in 1982, as part of Victoria's effort to reintroduce koalas across the state. The population grew from seventy-six koalas to ten thousand, according to Parks Victoria, the state agency that oversees national parks. Officials fear the trees will die and the koalas will starve.

In 1999, the state began relocating koalas from Mount Eccles to reduce the population. In May 2000, park rangers in Mount Eccles National Park coaxed more than one thousand koalas from the Manna Gum trees. The koalas were moved to other national and state parks in Victoria. "This program will prevent any irreparable damage by overbrowsing to the park and ensure the survival of the koala," said Ian Walker, chief ranger at Parks Victoria, in *The Age* by Richard Baker. However, state officials are concerned that there is a decreasing availability of suitable sites to release koalas in Victoria. This poses a major problem for the future of the Mount Eccles' koalas, whose population continues to grow.

A worker from Koala Rescue holds a koala who will be transported to a habitat with more abundant food sources.

Preventing overpopulation before it occurs

Because koala overpopulation is such a serious problem, and the solutions are expensive and time-consuming, people are trying to find ways to prevent overbrowsing from occurring in the first place. In Victoria, the government launched a public information campaign to alert people to the potential for koala overpopulation. Citizens are advised by Natural Resources and Environment, Victoria, the state environmental agency, to heed signs of koala overpopulation. The agency advises that koalas should be relocated before half of the trees of the preferred species have been depleted of foliage. Landowners are encouraged to place collars around tree trunks to discourage koalas from establishing home territories in areas without enough available trees.

The long-term solution to overpopulation is ensuring that koalas have adequate, protected habitats. More habitat restoration and conservation is needed to avert crowding too many koalas into limited areas. Rather than focusing on fertility control and translocation, the AKF recommends that public resources be spent on saving eucalyptus forests and preserving wildlife corridors so that koalas are able to move safely within their home ranges.

4

Protecting
Koala Habitat

As KOALA HOME ranges become smaller and more fragmented, overpopulation is likely to become an increasing problem for koalas. If the koala is to escape the dual threats of local extinction and overcrowding, advocates for the animal say that it is critical to restore and preserve koala habitat. Yet competition for land is intense in Australia, as it is around the world, making habitat preservation increasingly difficult to accomplish.

Compromises between environmentalists, who want to preserve forests and woodlands, and businesses, which seek to use the natural resources for profit, are often difficult and take many years to accomplish. Still, Australians are recognizing that the conservation of eucalyptus woodlands can have positive consequences reaching far beyond a single koala colony. Increasingly, people in many sectors of Australian society are working together to make this happen.

Protecting the environment

Early Australian conservationists mounted many protests to protect wilderness and wildlife in the first decades of the twentieth century. There was a wave of conservationist victories, including the rescue of the Blue Gum Forest, a eucalyptus forest with koalas in the Blue Mountains near Sydney, from logging in 1931. But after World War II, Australia entered a period of economic expansion, with growth in mining, forestry, livestock grazing, and urbanization. During this era of growth, koala habitat disappeared rapidly as cities and industries replaced hardwood forests and woodlands.

In the 1970s, environmentalist movements began to criticize the rapid, unrestrained development and loss of Australia's flora and fauna. Efforts by concerned citizens to preserve wilderness areas, protest logging in ancient forests, and protect endangered species continue today, as Australia tries to balance economic needs with ecological preservation. The push to protect koala habitat grew in the 1980s. During the 1990s, organizations such as the AKF became influential in advocating for koala forest preservation at the national level.

Slowing down logging

Conservationists have fought in recent decades to reduce logging and preserve key habitat of koalas in ancient forests. Many state forests harbor koala populations as well as other wild animals. However, the public forests are intended for multiple uses, such as logging, some of which conflict with the welfare of koalas. There is growing recognition that saving forests from clear-cutting will help not just koalas but other wildlife as well, and improve the quality of air and water.

The efforts of conservationists to reduce logging in koala habitats will improve the quality of air and water as well.

Conflicts over forests have occurred across southeast Australia. In the late 1990s, environmentalists protested the logging in the Strzelecki Ranges in Gippsland, Victoria. One of Victoria's most prized forest regions is located about one hundred miles southeast of Melbourne. The area includes eucalyptus forests, as well as rain forests that have long been converted to farmland and pine plantations, and some protected parks. Most of the region is controlled by timber companies, which are allowed to log the trees.

Yet Strzelecki is home to key populations of koalas. These koalas are very important because they are native to the region and are genetically unique from other Victorian koalas that were translocated from other parts of Australia and are not original inhabitants of this range.

Koala advocates are working hard to preserve the native habitat for the Strzelecki and South Gippsland koalas. In 1997 and 1998, Amcor, a paper company, proposed to clear 7,487 acres of koala habitat, potentially affecting an estimated population of two thousand koalas. Conservationists, including the nonprofit group Environment Victoria, launched protests to stop the logging. "Two thousand koalas could die, and these are a large part of the remaining endemic koala population in Victoria. . . . There is no justification for turning these forests into woodchips,"[23] said Dr. Rod Anderson of Environment Victoria.

Eventually, a team of environmental consultants was hired by the Victorian government to determine which part of the land should be preserved for wildlife. The end result was that a significant area of koala habitat was saved. In October 2000, the AKF made an agreement with the Hancock Timber Resources Group, a timber company that controls much of the region, to begin field studies to learn more about koalas and where they lived in the area. This is an example of how cooperation between koala advocates, the state government, and industry can save koalas, while allowing for economic growth.

Cooperation and compromise

In an effort to balance the economic needs of the timber industry with the environmental protection of the forests,

International Involvement

Saving koala habitat sometimes takes the support of international conservation projects. In 2000, an important piece of koala habitat was permanently protected by an international program to preserve natural areas. The Greater Blue Mountains Area, with expansive eucalyptus woodlands and significant koala habitat, was selected for the World Heritage Program, overseen by the United Nations Educational, Scientific, and Cultural Organization (UNESCO). As of 2000, Australia had fourteen properties on the World Heritage List.

The Greater Blue Mountains Area has long been a favorite of environmental groups. This area of 2.5 million acres of forest on a sandstone plateau, located 60 to 180 kilometers inland from Sydney in New South Wales, includes large expanses of wilderness, including seven national parks. The area is considered by arborists to be very important for encompassing a diversity of eucalyptus habitats, including swamps, wetlands, grasslands, and heaths. Some ninety-one species of eucalyptus grow there, offering safe refuge for koalas; studies are under way now to determine how many koalas still live in the area. With the international designation, new management plans are being put in place to identify specific pressures facing the region and to conserve the natural areas.

in the 1990s, the Australian states began to create Regional Forest Agreements to manage forests for twenty-year terms. The agreements allow logging in exchange for protection of some land as wilderness to protect biodiversity and old-growth trees. Advocates for koalas hope that the agreements will mean more protection for the animals.

Some agreements have been extremely controversial, while others have gained acceptance among both industry representatives and environmentalists. The Eden Regional Forest Agreement in New South Wales was criticized by conservationists for failing to protect key koala habitat. Under the agreement, logging will be allowed in the Murrah State Forest, which has a large breeding koala population, according to the Wilderness Society. In contrast, the South-East Queensland Forest Agreement gained widespread approval from conservationists for preserving key wildlife habitat, including koala habitat, while encouraging the timber industry to rely on plantations for wood resources.

In recent years, the management of state forests is emphasizing sustainable forestry, or allowing trees to grow to a certain height before cutting them down. Since taller, older trees are the best habitat for koalas and other wildlife, forests managed in this way will enable the survival of native wild animals. Efforts to label and market timber that comes from sustainable forests will help increase the practicality of forest conservation, since many people are now eager to buy environmentally friendly wood products. These endeavors will make a difference for koalas and other wildlife in the state forests.

Meanwhile, innovative koala management plans are becoming more common in forests with koala populations. In the Pine Creek State Forest, near Coffs Harbour in New South Wales, a group comprised of the timber industry, state forest, National Parks and Wildlife Service, and local residents, developed a koala management plan in 2000 to protect the approximately 450 koalas living in the forest. The plan is designed to sustain the population, while continuing to allow timber harvesting in parts of the forest where koalas are not living. Important koala habitat will be left untouched, and other areas will be planted with koala food trees. Thus, the timber industry is able to thrive, even while the koalas are protected.

Tree plantations

Future lumber needs can be at least partially met by growing young eucalyptus trees on plantations rather than cutting native forests and displacing the wildlife. Eucalyptus plantations are a growing industry in Australia. Plantation trees take four to fifteen years to mature, depending on irrigation, fertilizer, and the wood's use; trees harvested for pulp do not have to be as mature as trees used for hardwood products. Harvesting wood from plantations, rather than from forests, may help relieve the pressure on native forests. The Wilderness Society, an opponent of logging native forests, states that existing plantations are able to supply all of Australia's domestic timber needs, with the plantation estate expected to triple in size within the next twenty years.

At present, Australia has about 3.2 million acres of plantations; about 29 percent are eucalyptus plantations.

However, not everyone agrees that eucalyptus plantations can be considered an alternative to forests. Plantations do not generally provide appropriate habitat for koalas or other wildlife common to a native forest. Plantations usually grow only a few types of trees in a controlled environment, thus they cannot promote the biodiversity of a native forest. They can also cause their own environmental problems by taking up large tracts of land that might otherwise grow natural vegetation.

New farming techniques

Meanwhile, koalas continue to lose habitat to agriculture and grazing. The Pioneer Valley in Mackay on the central Queensland coast once encompassed a significant area of koala food trees. Now it has been almost completely cleared for sugarcane farming. In much of the region, no trees were left standing when the cane was planted.

Through education, financial incentives, and innovative agricultural methods, Australian farmers are learning to make profits, while preserving wild habitat and protecting the soil from becoming degraded. Since much of the koala's remaining habitat is in trees left standing along roads, along creeks bordering farms, and roads alongside rural property, efforts to educate farmers and livestock owners on land conservation and preservation will improve the future for koalas in agricultural regions.

A movement to encourage farmers to practice sustainable land use has flourished since the 1990s in Australia. Sustainable land use means that the fertility and natural features of a tract of land are maintained even while the land is used for crops and livestock. Land-use experts emphasize that sustainable land use can lead to better soil fertility and more profits

A growing industry of eucalyptus tree plantations saves native forests from destruction.

for the landowner, while at the same time retaining habitat for native wildlife like the koala.

Techniques that help preserve the quality of the land include rotating crops so that the soil nutrients are preserved, controlling weeds and pest animals such as rabbits which harm crops and remnant woodlands, and regularly moving sheep and cattle so that the animals do not overgraze the fields. Planting trees around the edges of fields helps farmers maintain good drainage and soil fertility, and benefits koalas and other wildlife that rely on these woodland patches.

In parts of New South Wales, farmers are given grants by local governments to build fences to conserve native vegetation on their property. Fences help keep grazing animals away from eucalyptus woodlands, where they may damage the trees by feeding near the roots. In some communities, farmers and other landowners receive financial incentives for agreeing to manage an area for nature conservation; that is, not allowing any activities that would harm native plants or wildlife like the koala. In one city in Victoria, farmers are given a tax rebate on land that is taken out of production because of tree and pasture planting, thus encouraging the preservation of native woodlands. Other communities, such as Caloundra City in Queensland, offer equipment, support

Farmers help solve koala habitat problems by planting trees around the edges of fields and keeping livestock away from eucalyptus woodlands.

from city workers, and even plants to residents who decide to revegetate their property.

Dryland salinity, or salt in the groundwater and soil, is a serious problem in Australia. It damages not only agricultural land and forests, but also roads, buildings, and playing fields. Soil salinity occurs when salt, which naturally occurs in rocks and sand on the soil's surface, dissolves and seeps into the groundwater, poisoning crops and drinking water. Farmers are encouraged to practice agricultural techniques that reduce soil salinity. These include planting salt tolerant trees, providing proper drainage so that excess water does not soak into the soil and dissolve salt into the groundwater, not overtilling the land, and keeping the land covered with vegetation. Vegetation on the land helps to soak up excess water so that it does not raise the water table and bring salt to the surface.

For example, farmers around Gunnedah in New South Wales have been planting native eucalyptus trees, which consume sixty or more gallons of water a day, to lower the water table and return salt-encrusted pasture to fertility, according to the *National Geographic*. "Save the soil, save the farmers, and save the koalas. A magic combination,"[24] said Dan Lunney of the New South Wales Park Service.

Preserving land and water resources

Farmers are realizing that conservation can benefit their businesses by preserving land and water resources. One in three farmers have voluntarily joined the forty-five hundred landcare groups in Australia. These groups, organized by the National Landcare Program, funded by the National Heritage Trust, look for ways to conserve Australia's land, vegetation, rivers, biodiversity, coasts, and seas. Farmers receive financial support—from tax incentives to the right to develop parts of their land if they set aside other areas for conservation—while learning to manage their land for conservation. With financial and technical support from the program, in the Gippsland area of Victoria, southeast of Melbourne, hundreds of farmers are planting trees along creeks and roads to help fight erosion and salinity. These trees provide koala habitat as well.

New restrictions on land and water use have created an economic burden for some farmers.

Not all the conservation measures are voluntary, however. New regulations and restrictions on water use and land clearance have caused some farmers to face a financial burden for the sake of conservation. Farmers' groups have protested that they are not adequately compensated for setting aside native vegetation and the loss of potentially productive land. They have asked for more financial assistance, such as lower taxes, for conservation projects that may cause them to lose money at first.

Planning for koalas in the suburbs

In urban and suburban regions, local governments play an important role in habitat preservation for koalas through their capacity to approve or deny development plans for new roads, businesses, and housing. Many communities are protecting koala habitat by asking, and in some cases requiring, developers to plant eucalyptus trees, or to build around, rather than through, a eucalyptus woodland. Voluntary tax rebates for private landowners to rezone their land for conservation have been instituted in Logan City, in southeast Queensland, which contains nationally significant koala habitat. No development or clearing can occur in these conservation areas. Developers and landowners receive up to a 50 percent tax rebate for conserving and restoring this land.

With the listing of the koala as "vulnerable" in New South Wales, communities in the state are required to take steps to protect the animal's habitat. In 1995, the state introduced a Koala Habitat Protection plan with guidelines for protecting areas with koalas. For example, when a proposed development or an activity, such as a new shopping center, is likely to have an effect on a koala population, a species impact statement, or a report on how the development will affect koalas living in the area, is required before government approval can be granted. If the project threatens to disrupt a koala colony, it may have to be modified.

Changing the zoning code to prohibit harmful activities on land occupied by koalas was accomplished in Port Stephens, a region on the central coast of New South Wales. The local koala population is estimated to number between several hundred to one thousand or more. But residential development, dog attacks, bush fires, and sand mining, or removing vegetation and dredging sandy areas for minerals, now pose significant threats to the animals. The patchy koala habitat is now 25 percent of what it was historically. To save the koalas, local authorities drew up a Koala Management Plan, which includes tree planting, traffic management, and other protective measures. The plan also recommends that parts of the Port Stephen's Tillegerry Peninsula, an area with a large koala population, be given Special Environmental Protection status, which means prohibiting sand mining or any other industrial activity that would disrupt the koalas.

Wildlife corridors

Another important feature to koala management in developed areas is providing the animals with strips of wild habitat to link koala home ranges. Grazing animals like koalas need safe passages between larger areas of woodlands so that young males can move to establish new territories and all koalas can find new food trees, if necessary. In developed areas, koalas have to cross dangerous roads or wander through backyards or parking lots to get to new eucalyptus trees. Habitat corridors, or strips of undeveloped land linking two larger pieces of koala habitat, allow the animals to move safely from place to place.

Fortunately for the koala, land clearing in Australia has often left behind the trees that grow next to rivers, since maintaining vegetation around rivers helps prevent soil erosion and keeps the water clean. "In many areas strips of eucalyptus forest have been retained as a defense against soil erosion, as windbreaks, as shade trees along rivers and streams or as part of the roadside verge [a planted strip of land at the edge of a road],"[25] writes koala expert Bill Phillips. These riverside habitats, often with a variety of gum trees, are favorite grazing places for koalas.

Designing a wildlife corridor

Communities are working to create habitat corridors for koalas. Developers are asked, and in some parts of Australia they are required, to include habitat corridors in their plans for new residential or industrial projects. In Pine Rivers Shire in southeast Queensland, developers must leave intact areas that have been identified as passageways. Then they are required to put up signs labeling the areas as "koala corridors." In New South Wales, efforts are underway to preserve a ribbon of undeveloped coastal land to link parks and wildlife refuges. This would not only help the wild animals in the area, but would also prevent coastal urban sprawl from overwhelming the scenic area.

Because koalas generally live in stable colonies on home ranges within certain boundaries, the wildlife corridors have to be carefully designed. As koala advocate Ann Sharp observes, koalas live within the boundaries of their home range, and will only move to new food trees within their home range. "A strip of vegetation will rarely incorporate the home range of one animal, let alone a whole population,"[26] she notes. The corridors need to include the home ranges of the individual koalas in the area, since koalas become very attached to their personal territory. The wildlife corridors must include food trees, and lead to new areas with food trees.

Koala reserve

One way to help koalas is to set aside reserves for the purpose of maintaining koalas and other local wildlife. In Redland Shire and Logan City, near Brisbane, the capital of Queensland, a remnant bushland with a history of koala habitation has been the focus of intense efforts to create a safe refuge for the animal. The Brisbane region contains an estimated several thousand koalas, which makes it one of the most significant koala regions in Australia. Because there are so many koalas, large areas of suitable habitat are needed to feed them.

A few hundred koalas in the Brisbane region have found sanctuary in the Koala Bushland Coordinated Conservation Area, thanks to the cooperative, voluntary efforts of many people. Urban sprawl was threatening this significant koala population in the early 1990s, so conservationists decided to forge an agreement among a variety of landowners to manage an area specifically for koalas. This area contains a state forest, national park, and local reserves, including open forests and woodlands with a large variety of eucalyptus. The landowners include public agencies and private individuals.

Eighty percent of the koala population live on private land.

Under the management policy for the conservation area, all the landowners have agreed to protect the land for koalas. No activities are allowed on the land that would threaten the koalas or their habitat. Visitors may picnic, observe wildlife, hike, ride horses on marked trails, and drive on designated roads. Educational activities, and even commercial ventures, such as bee-keeping, are allowed, but activities that cause stress or danger to koalas, such as riding motorbikes, camping, or removing native plants, are prohibited.

Protecting private land for koalas

An estimated 80 percent of all koalas live on privately owned land, according to the AKF. Private land has far

Koalas in National Parks

One way that nations protect their natural areas and wildlife is by setting aside land in national parks. In 1879, Australia declared the first national park, Royal National Park near Sydney, which encompasses eucalyptus forests and, historically, koalas. By 1916, every Australian state had at least one national park. Koalas have found refuge in some of Australia's five hundred national parks, which are generally large areas designated to protect native plants and animals. The parks offer public education and recreation, and usually include visitor facilities.

Australia's system of national parks and other preserves protects about 7.5 percent or 580,000 square kilometers [223,940 square miles] of undeveloped land from development. This is a small percentage of Australia's land, but one that is significant because it is fully protected. The use of the land within the parks is strictly regulated to protect the natural features of the area. State governments manage the national parks by setting park policy, providing staff, and developing conservation programs for the plants and wildlife. Many of the parks encompass the eucalyptus forests of Queensland, New South Wales, and Victoria, the core of the koala's range.

A koala clings to a eucalyptus tree in a wildlife-protected national forest in Australia.

fewer protections than public land because landowners are generally allowed to use their land as they wish. Thus, if koala habitat is to be protected on private land, landowners must voluntarily decide to manage their land in a way that does not conflict with koalas. In the past, landowners had little motivation to save koala habitat, especially if the habitat preservation interfered with their business, such as raising cattle or cotton.

The Australian government is taking steps to encourage private landowners to protect their land for wildlife. Through tax rebates and other incentives, private landowners are finding new benefits in preserving and planting eucalyptus trees. In Queensland, the government created a Land for Wildlife program, which is a voluntary conservation agreement designed to encourage landowners to establish wildlife habitat on their property. Landowners are given educational materials about the benefits of preserving wildlife habitat, such as controlling erosion and salinity. Since 1998, a total of 24,700 acres of private land, including eucalyptus woodlands, has been registered and saved in this program.

Very often, local, small-scale environmental efforts yield popular results. Tree planting is a hands-on activity, which does not cost much, or require too much labor, yet can reestablish koala habitat. Australia has promoted tree planting since the early 1980s, when the National Tree Program was established to begin reversal of two centuries of tree clearing. Farmers in all the states have organizations to promote and organize tree planting programs in rural areas. Citizens in suburbs and cities have also launched planting projects. Millions of trees have been planted in these programs, benefiting farmers by reducing soil erosion and salinity levels, while providing habitat for wildlife in the suburbs.

However, tree planting is a long-range project, since gum trees take at least fifteen years, sometimes thirty, to grow tall enough to be suitable as food trees for koalas. In addition, tree planting efforts have to be well planned if they are going to benefit koalas. People must consider carefully what types of trees koalas prefer in the local range. Also, the trees should be planted in existing home ranges of koalas so that they will be accessible to the local animals.

Mapping koala habitats

In the future, planning for koalas will be a lot easier because of the extraordinary efforts of the AKF. In the 1990s, this nonprofit group of volunteers began a major project to identify and map all remaining koala habitats in Australia. This information is being used to help communities become better educated about the koala's habitat needs and locations.

To gather information, the project uses field surveys and computer mapping to identify where koalas live and what types of trees they eat. Volunteers count koalas by searching for scat under trees that have been used by koalas. They can also tell koalas are in the area when they see the animal's characteristic scratches on smooth barked gum trees. Volunteers also use radio collars to track koalas in order to determine the extent of their ranges.

Koala Habitat Atlas

By early 2001, the AKF had mapped over 2.47 million acres and assessed nearly sixty thousand trees from around one thousand field sites across the east coast of Australia. "We believe that mapping is crucial because it puts the 'horse before the cart,'" said Sharp. "Koala habitat needs protecting right now. Not until you know where the most important koala habitat is can you do your best to protect it."[27] Once core areas of koala habitat are identified, then communities will be able to create master plans for towns and regions to prevent encroachment on koala habitat and interconnect pockets of habitat with corridors of eucalyptus trees in developed areas

The Koala Habitat Atlas is being used to plan for koala protection in Noosa Shire, Queensland, a premier tourist destination and an important koala habitat. About thirty koalas live in Noosa National Park, a protected area, but many more live in western parts of Noosa Shire on private land threatened by subdivision and development. "There is a perception that there are millions of koalas in the Park (because a million people see the same individual koalas over and over) and that they will be safe forever. This is far from reality,"[28] said Sharp. The AKF completed a Koala Habitat Atlas of the Noosa area in 2000, and presented it to the mayor of Noosa and the local council, the government

Hawks Nest and Tea Gardens Koalas

Among the most vulnerable koala populations in Australia in 2001 are those in Hawks Nest and Tea Gardens in New South Wales. With the population dipping very low, the state government decided in 1999 that the koalas in this region met the criteria of an endangered population. According to the Australian Koala Foundation (AKF) at that time, there were just twelve koalas living in the region.

Hawks Nest and Tea Gardens lie at the southern end of the Myall River, which flows from the Myall Lakes region of New South Wales. This system of coastal lakes bordered by sand dunes and beaches offers important habitat for sea birds, rain forest animals, and marsupials, including koalas, eastern grey kangaroos, swamp wallabies, and common ringtail possums. But loss of trees, road deaths, and nutritional stress brought on by diminished habitat has taken a toll on the koalas. Most land occupied by koalas in the area is currently zoned residential.

Koala advocates are concerned that more be done to protect the koala's habitat in the region and that a recovery plan be implemented for the population. "The Hawks Nest/Tea Gardens koala population is protected on paper by the strongest set of environmental laws currently existing in Australia, but in reality nothing has happened as yet to protect their trees or alleviate the daily threats of tree loss through ongoing development," said Deborah Tabart, executive director of the AKF. Conservationists and koala advocates are working hard to bring public attention and government action to this dwindling population of koalas.

body responsible for planning decisions. The Noosa government expects to use the atlas to develop a strategy for protecting koalas in the area. "The koala's future in Noosa is bleak, but with the Council's support we will be in a position to write a management plan for not only the National Park, but the whole Shire,"[29] said Sharp.

Balancing act

Saving the koala's habitat requires cooperation between people with different priorities and needs. Unless economic growth can accompany wild lands preservation, koalas will not get the widespread support they need to survive. Deborah Tabart of the AKF often says that land-use planning is the key to the koala's future. Loss of habitat inevitably leads to extinction, first of local populations, then of the species. Koala advocates and, increasingly, government officials, farmers, and community planners are helping to make sure that this never happens.

More incentives for landowners to save koala habitat and stricter conservation laws for public land are among the actions urged by koala advocates. Already, farmers are recognizing that planting eucalyptus trees helps retain topsoil, and city planners are realizing that retaining a wildlife corridor is good, not only for wildlife, but also for water quality and tourism. Often, saving a piece of land—or a single koala—is the necessary first step. Australia has an enthusiastic force of koala volunteers willing to take those initial steps toward saving koalas in their own backyards.

5

Keeping Koalas Safe in the Wild

WHILE SOME PEOPLE are working to preserve and expand the koala's wild habitat, others are trying to ensure the koala's health and safety in regions where it lives today. Wildlife experts and ordinary citizens alike, are assisting the koala to survive—and thrive—in a changing world. These efforts have grown into a koala protection movement, fueled largely by thousands of volunteers.

Beginning in the 1970s, when wildlife experts began noticing that the koala was suffering from diseases and struggling to survive in the wild, efforts to save the animal have occurred on many fronts. Scientists are learning more about koala behavior and what the koala needs to survive in the wild. Local and state governments are also taking steps to save koala colonies and reduce conflicts with humans. Communities are learning how to keep koalas safe in a home range that might span eucalyptus woodlands and suburban backyards.

Often, it is people in the community who first notice that a koala colony is in trouble. "People on the ground see koala habitat being cleared and alert us. Without the ordinary citizens, many of whom are extraordinary people, the crucial information would be almost impossible to gather,"[30] said Ann Sharp. This knowledge often spurs local groups to push for stronger environmental laws to protect koalas and their habitat.

Koala volunteers

Reducing the impact of human activity on koalas is the focus of koala volunteers. Koala care groups have formed in many cities and towns to rescue the sick, injured, and orphaned koalas who wander into communities. "These people dedicate their lives to rescuing, rehabilitating and returning koalas to the wild. They also educate the people in their local districts about the dangers that koalas face, such as cars, dogs and development,"[31] says Sharp.

Citizens in the Mornington Peninsula Shire on the coast of Victoria were instrumental in helping to protect local koalas from loss of habitat and food trees. The region includes a variety of koala habitats, including eucalyptus woodlands on French Island and Phillip Island, and small patches, mostly on a naval base, on the mainland peninsula. Citizens joined with politicians and wildlife experts to figure out how best to protect the koalas.

As a result, the community helped to plant trees, created a koala management plan, and preserved land for koalas. They formed a local koala advocacy group, Friends of Local Koalas Lands and Wildlife, which has sent people out to count koalas to get a better grasp of the population and where it lives. Meanwhile, Parks Victoria is creating a wildlife corridor on the mainland peninsula.

Rescuing an injured koala

When it comes to handling koalas, volunteers are extremely cautious. Koalas are wild animals; when they are scared, they will bite and scratch people who hold them. Because of this, state wildlife officials, trained in animal welfare, are the first people to step in to rescue koalas found injured on the roadside. Yet since so many koalas need help in numerous communities, wildlife agencies have come to rely on volunteers to assist them.

Volunteers who care for koalas need a permit from state wildlife authorities because koalas are considered protected wild animals and it is against the law to capture or keep them without a permit. Volunteers must take a training course to learn how to rescue and care for joeys and koalas. They learn how to give koalas the highly specialized care they need to be rehabilitated and eventually returned to the wild.

For example, a person who is rescuing an injured koala should use a sturdy pair of gloves to handle the animal. It is best to wrap the koala in a bag or blanket to keep it warm. Then, people are advised to place it in a basket or box and allow it to rest quietly, since excessive handling can shock and even kill the animal. (Since koalas are extremely sensitive to being handled, they can quickly become ill as a result of stress caused by direct human contact.) A pressure bandage can be used to stop bleeding, and fractured limbs should be secured to the koala's body. Often, communities use local tax dollars to fund a wildlife ambulance and veterinarian to pick up koalas who are injured on the roadside.

Once trained professionals gather injured koalas, volunteers step in to help care for the animals. Raising an injured or orphaned koala is demanding. The young koalas need frequent feeding and constant attention. Very young joeys have to be fed a milk formula about every two to four

A volunteer worker feeds a rescued joey with a dropper.

hours from a dropper. They are also fed pulverized euca-lyptus leaves. Sometimes the joeys sleep in the same bed as the caretaker while being fed formula and leaves. Grad-ually, the tiny joeys must be weaned off human contact and allowed to mix with other young koalas, so that later they will be able to survive on their own.

Jenny Bryant, a koala carer (as caregivers are called) in Lismore, Victoria, described her experiences in the newslet-ter of a local koala group: "At present I have a mother koala with a male baby about nine months old. She had been attacked by two large dogs and suffered injuries to her head and neck. She was extremely distressed and in shock. . . . After days of feeding her fluids by syringe, plus various injections, she has started eating leaves and looks more alert. She still has a long way to go, but is looking hopeful. Her baby is doing well, and throughout her ordeal has cared for him perfectly."[32] Putting in hours of time and energy, koala carers have saved thousands of individual koalas that would have died.

Koala hospitals

Spurred by volunteer enthusiasm and financial dona-tions, hospitals devoted to the care of sick and injured koalas have sprung up across southeast Australia. While the hospitals do have staff veterinarians, much of the hands-on care for the koalas is accomplished by armies of round-the-clock volunteers. Many of the hospitals were begun by groups of citizens, who started by caring for koalas in their homes, then realized that more specialized medical care was needed by the growing number of or-phaned and injured koalas found by the roadside.

In 1972, in the town of Port Macquarie on the coast of the Tasman Sea in New South Wales, a couple named Jean and Max Starr, local shopkeepers, organized the Koala Preservation Society of New South Wales, supported en-tirely by volunteers. As Ken Phillips described in his 1994 book, *Koalas: Australia's Ancient Ones*, the group hoped to save habitat, educate people about the koala, and rescue and treat the sick and injured animals.

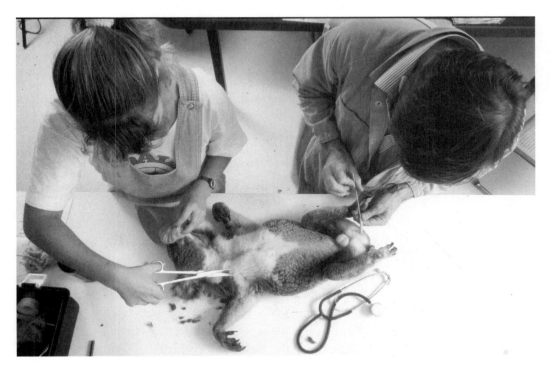

At first, members cared for injured koalas in their own homes, collecting food leaves each morning before dawn. The first patient was a koala who was totally blind from conjunctivitis. Because little was known about koala diseases and how to treat them, the koala soon died. But other koalas followed. As more was learned about treating koala diseases, the group was able to save many koalas.

The group built a small hospital in the 1970s. Then with funds raised through local raffles, they built the Koala Hospital in 1986. The hospital includes yards with eucalyptus trees and intensive care units, with X-ray and anesthesia machines. Volunteer rescue units bring in the koalas, found wandering on roads, often with fractured bones or internal injuries from car accidents.

Sick or injured koalas are treated by veterinarians who perform surgery and prescribe medicine. But much of the nonmedical care is still provided by volunteers. Some of the koalas die because they have been too seriously injured or do not eat well in captivity, while others are eventually

A rescued koala receives treatment in a veterinary hospital.

released to the wild. The koalas are given an opportunity to learn and improve climbing and jumping skills so that they will survive when returned to the wild. Between 150 and 200 koalas are treated at the Koala Hospital in Port Macquarie each year. By 1990, the volunteers had cared for over two thousand koalas. During the bush fires of 1994, 80 koalas were rescued and treated at this hospital.

Reducing suburban hazards

Educating the public about koala health and safety is another emphasis of many community-based koala groups. Koalas wandering into the suburbs face perils all around. Teaching residents how to help koalas avoid dangerous situations will reduce the numbers of injured and orphaned koalas.

Public awareness campaigns focus on practical solutions to the koala's problems in urban and suburban areas. For example, owners of swimming pools can keep a stout rope dangling in the pool so that if a koala falls in, the animal can catch on to the rope and climb out. People can choose to build koala-friendly fences (with spaces for passage and easy-to-grip material) in their backyards, which allow koalas to climb over them without injury. To avoid conflicts with domestic dogs, people are advised to restrain their pets on a leash or rope, especially at night when koalas may be on the ground moving from tree to tree. These simple actions can save the lives of many koalas.

State and local initiatives

Meanwhile, state and local governments are taking steps to protect koalas. Across southeastern Australia, wildlife warning signs such as "Koala Crossing" have been posted by local and state governments to alert drivers to the possibility of koalas on the road. In 1995, the Queensland Parks and Wildlife Service identified sections of roads with high numbers of koala deaths. These roads were targeted for lower speed limits during the evening hours between August and December, when most koala traffic deaths occur because of the koala mating season. In some places, officials posted signs that tallied the number of koalas that died on the roads.

In some communities, residents are required by law to restrain their household pets in order to reduce attacks on koalas and other wild animals. In Pine Rivers Shire, a mixture of rural and urban communities north of Brisbane, Queensland, with a substantial koala population, dog owners are required to keep their pets in enclosures or on leashes. Violators are fined up to $3,750 (Australian dollars). In the shire, 124 koala deaths were reported in one year, many caused by pet attacks.

In other regions, residents are willing to pay slightly more taxes to help their local koalas. Redland Shire, in southeastern Queensland, which is home to one of the major koala populations in the country, imposes an annual environmental tax to raise money to buy critical habitat for koalas and other wildlife. In the 1990s, the shire acquired part of Point Halloran peninsula in order to protect a koala colony. The shire also pays for public education about koala conservation, funds a wildlife ambulance to pick up injured koalas, and supports food tree planting in parks.

National koala conservation

Growing concern about the koala on the local level has encouraged Australia to focus new attention on the animal and its status in the wild. In 1985, the Australian National Parks and Wildlife Service began the Koala Conservation Program and launched a study to learn more about koalas and the conservation measures needed to protect them. A National Koala Survey was undertaken between 1985 and 1987, assisted by tens of thousands of ordinary citizens, to determine the koala's favored habitat and food trees, distribution, and prevalence of disease. The survey found that koalas were still widespread, but that loss of habitat posed the most serious risk to the species.

In 1998, the government published the National Koala Conservation Strategy, which sets management priorities for koalas. Developed by the Australian and New Zealand Environment and Conservation Council, the strategy addresses the needs of koalas in different parts of the country. The primary aim is to "conserve koalas by retaining viable populations in the wild throughout their natural range."[33] This includes six major objectives: To conserve koalas in their existing habitat; to rehabilitate and restore koala habitat and populations; to develop a better understanding of the conservation biology of koalas; to educate the public about the koala; to manage captive, sick, injured, and orphaned koalas with high standards of care; and to manage overbrowsing to prevent both koala starvation and ecosystem damage in patches of habitat. The responsibility for carrying out these objectives belongs to all levels of government, as well as to conservation agencies and community groups. However, some critics say that the strategy is not as effective as it could be, since the guidelines are general and compliance is mostly voluntary. Few penalties exist, except fines for killing koalas or damaging protected habitat in some parts of the country.

Meanwhile, koala volunteers and advocacy groups are lobbying for stronger koala protection laws. Thus far, management of the koala is left primarily up to the states and local communities, where laws vary widely. In April 2001, the Australian Koala Foundation (AKF) held a National Koala Act Summit to formulate a national plan for koala conservation. The act would establish tax incentives for landholders willing to protect koala habitat on their property. Also, the AKF wants the koala listed as threatened under the Environmental Protection and Biodiversity Conservation Act so that a national Koala Recovery Plan would be established. "If our government is prepared to make these concessions for the koalas, it would be a tremendous step towards genuine koala conservation,"[34] said Tabart.

Koala refuges

While koala advocates work to strengthen conservation laws for koalas in the wild, most people will never see a koala in a native eucalyptus woodland. Instead, they will learn about koalas by reading about them or seeing them in captivity. Across the koala's range, numerous parks and refuges harbor koalas in protected habitats. These refuges

International Protection for the Koala

On June 8, 2000, the United States listed the koala as a threatened species under the U.S. Endangered Species Act (ESA) citing habitat destruction as the primary threat to the survival of koalas. (The ESA was passed by Congress in 1973 to protect plants and animals from extinction.) "Despite several conservation actions by the Government of Australia and State governments, the limited koala habitat continues to deteriorate," states the U.S. Fish and Wildlife Service in its Final Rule on the listing. It states that disease, loss of genetic variation, and death by dogs and motor vehicles due to development are secondary factors threatening koalas.

The koala listing is controversial in Australia. The Australian government objects to the assessment that the koala is a threatened species. Government officials have also expressed concern that the United States is interfering with the management of an Australian animal. In a *Reuters News Service* report, Australian environment minister Robert Hill said the listing was "inappropriate and unnecessary" and that the "U.S. decision will not contribute to the conservation of the species in Australia." He said that "it does not take into account the conservation and wildlife management strategies in place in Australia." Colin Griffiths, director of Australia's National Parks and Wildlife Service, submitted comments to the U.S. Fish and Wildlife Service, pointing out that the Australian government has determined the koala is not threatened. "We have yet to see any explanation of how the listing of the koala in the United States would contribute to koala conservation," he stated.

While the listing does not protect critical habitat because the koala is a foreign species, the United States is required to assist in koala conservation and recovery programs. Also, koalas are only allowed into the United States if they contribute to the conservation of the species. "It will force institutions to be more prepared to receive animals," says Valerie Thompson, who is the coordinator of the Koala Species Survival Plan in the United States, in an interview in January 2001. Thompson adds that the listing "sends a message to the Australian government about what the U.S. perspective is . . . it may be a motivator."

serve the dual purpose of conservation and education. Australians and tourists can actually see koalas and learn more about the marsupial in a natural environment. Learning more about koalas is a first step to supporting koala conservation in the wild.

Some reserves have been set up to protect specific koala populations. The Koala Conservation Centre, managed by the Phillip Island Nature Park, was established to save the dwindling population of koalas on Phillip Island in Victoria, and to educate the public about protecting the species. In recent decades, koalas were being killed on the roads and their habitat was being destroyed with the clearing of land for development, forcing the koalas to subsist on too few food trees. To protect the remaining koalas, the island created a safe haven for the animals, where people could learn about the hazards they face and what can be done to protect them.

Raising public awareness

The Koala Conservation Centre encompasses a small plantation of Manna Gums, Swamp Gums, and Blue Gums within a designated reserve area. Visitors can walk among the natural koala habitat and see koalas up in the trees where they live. They can learn the koala's problems, from loss of habitat and isolation to the hazards of suburban living.

Across Australia, hundreds of koalas live in captivity in zoos, wildlife parks, and reserves, where they are on display to the public. The commercial display of koalas can be useful to koala conservation in a number of ways, particularly in raising public awareness about the species and their challenges in the wild. The sweet-looking animal is, in a way, its own advertisement, for people often find it hard to resist the nonthreatening appeal of the koala.

At the Australian Wildlife Park in Sydney, for example, the koala collection is a popular stop for tourists. People are eager for a chance to glimpse the animal. At the same time, the park tries to educate visitors about the challenges now facing the marsupial. "Sadly, there is the potential of koalas becoming endangered in the wild. But our koalas can help us learn what it may take to save them," said the park's wildlife curator John Horton. "Our koalas are the best ambassadors. People came from around the world to see them. When they spend time with them, people know they're special animals worth saving,"[35]

Koalas in zoos help koalas in the wild

Koalas in captivity assist scientists in learning more about the animal's needs in the wild. The koala's diet is of particular interest. Early attempts to raise koalas in captivity failed because the koalas did not get the appropriate diet of fresh tree leaves. Koala carers tried different types of eucalyptus and other foods to see just what koalas will eat. They discovered that they had to find the particular species of eucalyptus that appealed to each individual animal. Sjoukje Vaartjes, who manages the Northern population of koalas in Australia's zoos, comments, "The greatest challenge is to be able to provide adequate eucalyptus branches for their diet."[36]

Only a few zoos outside Australia have been able to raise koalas successfully. The World Famous San Diego Zoo, run

Koalas raised in captivity help scientists understand their needs in the wild.

by the Zoological Society of San Diego, has been a leader in raising koalas in captivity in the United States. In the 1920s the zoo tried to raise koalas, but feeding the animals proved to be a problem. When the zoo acquired koalas again in the 1950s, it was much more successful. This time, the zoo imported koalas from the Lone Pine Koala Sanctuary outside Brisbane, and followed the sanctuary's management techniques.

The best solution to feeding koalas was for the zoo to grow its own eucalyptus trees. Thousands of eucalyptus seedlings are raised each year in the zoo's groves and a nearby nursery. Since koalas like certain trees more than others, each animal

A koala appears at home in this eucalyptus tree at the World Famous San Diego Zoo in California.

is given an individualized collection of fresh leaves. The koalas are offered fresh branches from several kinds of eucalyptus trees. They can select the kind they like best.

The zoo's koala collection is the largest koala colony outside Australia. More than eighty koalas are managed by the zoo, including a rare albino koala, named Onya-Birri ("ghost boy" in an aboriginal language) by the zoo, born in September 1997. Many of these koalas are on loan to zoos in North America and Europe. The money raised through the lending program is used to help fund koala research and habitat studies in Australia.

In addition, zoo staff participate in koala conservation efforts. Valerie Thompson, an assistant curator of mammals at the zoo who also manages the koala population in the United States for the American Zoo Association, has traveled to New South Wales to evaluate eucalyptus habitat and determine the conservation needs of the koala. She participated in the 2001 conference to develop the National Koala Act in Australia.

A rare albino koala called "Ghost Boy" holds tightly to another koala at the World Famous San Diego Zoo.

Koala's Sensitivity

Raising koalas in captivity is not easy, since koalas react poorly to unfamiliar situations, people, and surroundings. Associate Curator Valerie Thompson at the World Famous San Diego Zoo tries to create a stress-free environment for the zoo's koalas. The zoo staff who handle Blinky Bill, Tuckonie, Onya-Birri, and the other resident koalas strive for a consistent, predictable, and calm environment. "Koalas are animals that do react to unusual things they're not used to. Consistency is one of the keys to our successful program," said Thompson in a January 2001 interview with the author. "Everything about how we deal with koalas is based on being proactive to avoid stress."

Along with providing a specialized eucalyptus diet, the zoo created habitats for the koalas that are comfortable and familiar. Each koala has a custom-made perch on which to sit. The angle of the wood is carefully measured so that the koala can lean comfortably, as it would do in a real eucalyptus tree.

To avoid aggressive behavior, males and females are kept separate, unless a female displays signs of readiness to breed. Male koalas live alone, as they do in the wild. Females are more compatible and live in groups together, but the zoo segregates females with joeys from females without joeys. Joeys are nondiscriminatory about which koala female they climb on, so a female who is not a mother might not appreciate a joey climbing on her back.

Zookeepers begin handling the koalas when they are very young to get them used to being picked up. They use gloves and exercise extreme caution, because koalas scratch and bite when they are agitated. They perch them in the crook of their arms, mimicking the shape of the forking branch of a eucalyptus. Zookeepers are alert for health problems, because even minor illnesses can become serious for koalas. "A runny nose is a big problem, because they taste test the eucalyptus leaves by smelling them. If they can't smell, they won't eat," says Thompson.

Each year, some of the zoo's healthiest koalas are loaned to other zoos. Only koalas who seem able to make the transition are chosen. The koalas travel with a zookeeper by airplane. For the trip, the koalas travel in a sky kennel, equipped with a custom-made perch and plenty of eucalyptus leaves. "They're used to it. They ride in the passenger section next to the keeper," said Thompson.

Keeping a respectful distance

The koala's popularity sometimes leads to problems for the animal. In recent years, wildlife experts have questioned the common practice of allowing people to pick up or touch koalas in zoos or wildlife reserves. Koala caretakers have found that the koalas come under stress when they are handled. Although koalas look passive and cuddly, they are wild animals and are not used to being touched or held. Sometimes they bite or scratch people who are holding them. In addition, when koalas feel stressed, they are more susceptible to illness.

For these reasons, tourists are not allowed to hold koalas in some places. In New South Wales, tourists or spectators are prevented from having direct contact with a koala or to repeatedly remove a koala from an object it is clinging to. For a few years, koalas were placed on plush toys or cushions which were then passed to tourists to hold, but as of 1997 even this contact is no longer allowed. In other parts of Australia, handling koalas is permitted under supervision and appropriate standards.

People are working hard on many fronts to enable koalas, both in captivity and in the wild, to survive in a rapidly changing world. The threats facing the koala are serious. Yet with the help of new research and new ideas, people are coming up with innovative ways to protect the koala. Together, wildlife experts, government policy-makers, and community residents who share their land with koalas, are striving to give Australia's beloved koala a safe and secure future.

Koalas, sensitive to the stress of being handled, are best appreciated at a distance by humans.

Notes

Introduction

1. Ann Sharp, *The Koala Book*. Gretna, LA: Pelican Publishing, 1995, p. 79.

2. Quoted in Joni Praded, "The Koala Enigma," *Animals*, May 1999, p. 8.

Chapter 1: Life in a Eucalyptus Tree

3. Quoted in Bill Phillips, *Koalas: The Little Australians We'd All Hate to Lose*. Canberra: Australian Government Publishing Services, 1987, p. 18.

4. Simon Hunter, *The Official Koala Handbook*. London: Chatto & Windus, 1987, p. 41.

5. Ken Phillips, *Koalas: Australia's Ancient Ones*. New York: Macmillan, 1994, p. 88.

6. Sharp, *The Koala Book*, p. 88.

7. Quoted in W. Robinson, "Leukemia in Koalas: The Evidence for Viral Involvement," Koalas Diseases, www.onthenet.com.au/~jbergh/koala3.htm.

8. Roger Martin and Kathrine Handasyde, *The Koala: Natural History, Conservation and Management*. Malabar, FL: Krieger Publishing, 1999, p. 51.

Chapter 2: Vanishing Eucalyptus

9. Bill Phillips, *Koalas*, p. 25.

10. Martin and Handasyde, *The Koala*, p. 25

11. Bill Phillips, *Koalas*, p. 61

12. Bill Phillips, *Koalas*, p. 61

13. Mark Clayton, "Chipping Away at Australia's Old Growth Forests," *Christian Science Monitor*, May 24, 1996, p. 10.

14. Sharp, *The Koala Book*, p. 76.

15. Martin and Handasyde, *The Koala*, p. 27.

16. Martin and Handasyde, *The Koala*, p. 27.

17. Quoted in Jane Bennett, et al., *Watching Wildlife: Australia*. Melbourne, Australia: Lonely Planet Publications, 2000, p. 64.

Chapter 3: Islands and Overpopulation

18. Martin and Handasyde, *The Koala*, p. 68.

19. Quoted in CNN, "Koalas Overcrowded Down Under," November 30, 1996, http://cnn.com/EARTH/9611/30/koalas/ index.html.

20. Quoted in Geoff Spencer, "Kill Koalas? Controversy Engulfs 2,000 Cuddly Bears," Associated Press, March 19, 1996, http://detnews.com/menu/stories/40487.htm.

21. Quoted in Shawn Donnan, "Australia Tackles a Cute Conundrum," *Christian Science Monitor*, July 18, 2000, p. 7.

22. Quoted in Donnan, "Australia Tackles a Cute Conundrum," p. 7.

Chapter 4: Protecting Koala Habitat

23. Quoted in Environment Victoria, "Strzelecki Conflict over Forest, Clearing." www.lexicon.net/peterc/PAGES/STRZ.HTM.

24. Quoted in Oliver Payne, "Koalas Out on a Limb," *National Geographic*, April 1995, p. 58.

25. Bill Phillips, *Koalas*, p. 61.

26. Sharp, *The Koala Book*, p. 94.

27. E-mail interview with the author, February 8, 2001.

28. E-mail interview with the author, February 8, 2001.

29. E-mail interview with the author, February 8, 2001.

Chapter 5: Keeping Koalas Safe in the Wild

30. E-mail from Ann Sharp to author, January 25, 2001.

31. E-mail from Ann Sharp to author, January 25, 2001.

32. Quoted in Jenny Bryant, Wildlife Carer's Report, *Folklaw News*, Autumn 1998, http://home.vicnet.net.au/~folklaw/Knews~1.htm.

33. Quoted in Australian and New Zealand Environment and Conservation Council, National Koala Conservation Strategy, p. 7.

34. Quoted in Australian Koala Foundation, "National Koala Act," www.savethekoala. com/nka.html.

35. Quoted in Suzanne Herp, "Goodie Goodie Gumdrop," Australian Koala Foundation, www.akf.au/ More_Koala.html.

36. E-mail from Sjoukje Vaartjes to author, March 7, 2001.

37. Bill Phillips, *Koalas*, p. 3.

Glossary

Aborigine: Aborigine means "from the beginning"; Australia's indigenous people who came from Asia about fifty thousand years ago.

arboreal: Arboreal animals spend most of their life in trees.

biodiversity: The existence of a variety of plant and animal life in a particular habitat of the world.

browse: To eat leaves and parts of trees and shrubs.

the bush: The Australian word for wilderness.

caecum: Important part of the koala's digestive tract.

corridor: A band of vegetation, usually older forest, which connects distinct patches of forest.

cull: To kill wild animals in order to relieve overpopulation.

deforestation: The removal of a large number of trees from an area.

ecosystem: A community of interacting organisms and their physical environment.

endangered species: A plant or animal that is threatened with extinction.

eucalyptus: Any one of over seven hundred trees and shrubs in the genus *Eucalyptus*.

Eucalyptus: A genus of hard-leafed evergreen trees and shrubs native to Australia.

extinction: A species is extinct when no living members exist.

feral: An animal that is wild, such as the feral cat.

foliage: Leaves of a tree or other plant.

fragmented: Transformation of a large continuous forest into patches of forest surrounded by disturbed areas and human activity.

gum tree: Common Australian word for eucalyptus tree.

habitat: Natural living area of animals with a distinct plant community.

herbivore: An animal that eats only plants.

home range: The area in which an animal lives and moves over a lifetime.

joey: A young marsupial.

marsupial: Mammals without a placenta who give birth to undeveloped young, which nurse in the mother's pouch.

monotreme: Primitive egg-laying mammal, such as the platypus.

nocturnal: Active at night.

placenta: A membrane enclosing the fetus that exchanges oxygen, wastes, and nutrients between the mother's blood and the fetus.

predator: An animal who eats other animals.

prey: An animal who is hunted for food by other animals.

range: The area naturally occupied by a species.

salinity: Salt in the soil and water; rising groundwater brings salt with it, which can be harmful to plants.

sand mining: Australia's mineral sands contain valuable heavy metals. The sand mining industry excavates natural areas along Australia's east coast.

scent gland: Concentration of cells that secrete chemicals conveying information about the animal.

sclerophyll forest: Evergreen forest dominated by hard-leafed trees including eucalyptus.

species: A population of plants or animals distinguished from other such populations by certain characteristics.

stress: A reaction to adverse external or internal stimulus, which disturbs an animal's well-being.

threatened: A species that could become endangered if no steps are taken to protect it.

translocate: To place members of a species in a new habitat.

vasectomy: A surgical sterilization procedure performed on males.

vulnerable: A species that is at risk but not yet endangered.

woodland: A habitat where well-spaced trees grow within an open canopy.

Organizations to Contact

Australian Conservation Foundation
340 Gore St., Fitzroy Victoria 3065 Australia
03-9416-0767 • fax: 03-9416-0767
e-mail: acf@acfonline.org.au • website: www.acfonline.org.au

Australia's leading environmental group is involved in many activities to help protect native vegetation and preserve biodiversity in the country.

Australian Koala Foundation
GPO Box 2659, Brisbane Queensland 4001 Australia
61-7-3229 7233 • fax: 61-7-3221 0337
e-mail: akf@savethekoala.com • website: www.savethekoala.com
Toll Free in North America: 1-800-MYKOALA

The Australian Koala Foundation is a private, nonprofit organization. Its aim is the long-term conservation and effective management of the Koala in the wild.

Australians for Animals
PO Box 673, Byron Bay NSW 2481 Australia
website: www.australiansforanimals.org.au

This national advocacy group for Australia's wildlife has worked hard to draw the public's attention to the koala and its vanishing habitat.

Environment Australia
GPO Box 787, Canberra ACT 2601 Australia
61-2-6274-1111 • fax: 61-2-6274-1123
website: www.environment.gov.au

This is the government agency that oversees national policy and programs relating to conservation of wildlife and habitat. The website offers information about current programs in Australia to conserve wild animals and places. Also provides links to other information.

The Wilderness Society
130 Davey St., Hobart TAS 7000 Australia
03-6234-9799 • fax: 03-6224-1497
e-mail: info@wilderness.org.au • website: www.wilderness.org.au

This national environmental advocacy organization seeks to protect the future of the wilderness and conservation areas in Australia. Since 1976, the Wilderness Society has protected over 12.3 million acres of wilderness, including Kangaroo Island, with its koala populations.

World Wide Fund for Nature—Australia
WWF International
Ave du Mont-Blanc, CH 1196 Gland Switzerland
fax: 41-22-364-0074
website: www.wwf.org.au

This international, independent conservation organization with 4.7 million members in ninety-six countries works to preserve biodiversity by promoting sustainable use of natural resources. The WWF has been working in Australia for over twenty years to conserve species, reduce pollution, and protect wild areas. The WWF supports the Threatened Species Network, which educates the public about the recovery of threatened Australian species and their habitats.

Suggestions for Further Reading

Books

Jane Bennettet al., *Watching Wildlife: Australia*. Melbourne, Australia: Lonely Planet Publications, 2000. Wildlife and natural areas of Australia are explored by Australian writers, using detailed descriptions along with photographs and maps.

Encyclopedia of Mammals. Vol. 8. New York: Marshall Cavendish, 1997. The section on koalas, "Up a Gum Tree," describes the animal's physiology, diet, and life in the eucalyptus trees of southeastern Australia.

Simon Hunter, *The Official Koala Handbook*. London: Chatto & Windus, 1987. A book of facts about the koala's place in Australia's social history, literature, and eucalyptus forests.

Bill Phillips, *Koalas: The Little Australians We'd All Hate to Lose*. Canberra: Australian Government Publishing Service, 1987. The history and natural evolution of the koala and its habitat, using information from a survey of koalas by the Australian National Parks and Wildlife Service.

Ken Phillips, *Koalas: Australia's Ancient Ones*. New York: Macmillan, 1994. An American's experience learning about koalas and conservation efforts in one community in New South Wales.

Ambrose Pratt, *The Call of the Koala*. Melbourne, Australia: Robertson & Mullens, 1937. A study of the koala and its life and presence in Australia in the early twentieth century.

Ann Sharp, *The Koala Book*. Gretna, LA: Pelican Publishing, 1995. A look at the koala's evolution, life cycle, and socialization, with many color photographs.

John Vandenbeld, *Nature of Australia: A Portrait of the Island Continent*. New York: Facts On File, 1988. Photographs and descriptions of the rich diversity of wildlife in Australia.

Websites

Australia Down Under, http://library.thinkquest.org/28994/index.html. An award-winning website created by two eighth-graders provides a comprehensive look at Australian geography, history, culture, wildlife, and more.

Australian Koala Foundation, www.akfkoala.gil.com.au. This organization provides information and advocates for the conservation and management of koalas in the wild.

Australian Wildlife and Natural History, www.gullivermedia.com.au/wildlife.html. This website offers photographs and descriptions of the koala and its habitat, as well as other Australian wildlife and wild places.

Friends of the Koala, www.nor.com.au. Information about the group of volunteers that helps save koalas in the Lismore area of New South Wales.

Kangaroo Island Koala Rescue, www.npf.org.au/Why_rescue.html. A look at the process of catching and relocating koalas on Kangaroo Island, by the South Australia Department for Environment Heritage and Aboriginal Affairs.

The Koala Page, www.oms.berkeley.edu/~jpeng/Koala/koala.html. Information resource about koala physiology, diet, and behavior.

Koala Preservation Society, www.midcoast.com.au. The Koala Preservation Society is a group of volunteers that helps rescue injured koalas, runs the Koala Hospital, and saves koala habitat in a suburban region of New South Wales.

Koalas, www.thekoala.com/koala. General information about koalas.

Redlands Shire, www.redland.net.au. Redland Shire, in subtropical southeast Queensland, is home to one of the major koala populations in Australia. This website describes what is being done in Redlands Shire to protect the koala and save its habitat.

The World Famous San Diego Zoo, www.sandiegozoo.org/wildideas/animal/koala.html. The San Diego Zoo's experience with caring for koalas in captivity has helped other zoos do the same.

Video
The World of the Koala, Wildfilm Australia, 1995. An in-depth look at the koala and its life in the woodlands of Australia.

Works Consulted

Books

David Bergamini et al., *The Land and Wildlife of Australia*. New York: Time Life Books, 1964. A comprehensive description of Australia's geologic history and wildlife.

Scott Forbes, ed., *Australian Outback*. Singapore: Discovery Communications, 2000. Beautiful photographs of Australia's wild places.

Bernhard Grzimek, ed., *Grzimek's Encyclopedia of Mammals*. Vol. 1. New York: McGraw-Hill, 1990. A description of the koala's physiology and behavior.

Eric Hoffman, *Adventuring in Australia: A Sierra Club Travel Guide*. San Francisco: Sierra Club Books, 1999. A look at Australia's wildlife and natural places.

Robert Hughes, *The Fatal Shore: The Epic of Australia's Founding*. New York: Vintage Books, 1986. A history of the settlement of Australia as a British penal colony.

Roger Martin and Kathrine Handasyde, *The Koala: Natural History, Conservation and Management*. Malabar, FL: Krieger Publishing, 1999. A comprehensive overview of the koala and its management in the wild.

Denis O'Byrne, *South Australia*. Hawthorn, Victoria: Lonely Planet Publications, 1996. A traveler's guide to South Australia, with a stop at Kangaroo Island, home of koalas.

Roff Martin Smith, *The National Geographic Traveler: Australia*. Washington: National Geographic Society, 1999. A look at the history and natural wonders of Australia today.

Paul Theroux, *The Happy Isles of Oceania: Paddling the Pacific*. New York: Ballantine Books, 1992. The firsthand account of a journey through Australia and other parts of the Pacific, and the people and wildlife encountered there.

Periodicals

Australian and New Zealand Conservation Council, "National Koala Conservation Strategy," *Environment Australia*, January 1998.

Mona Chiang, "Australia's Amazing Animals," *Science World*, September 4, 2000.

Mark Clayton, "Chipping Away at Australia's Old Growth Forests," *Christian Science Monitor*, May 24, 1996.

"Conservation of Koalas in Australia," Special Section, *Conservation Biology*, June 2000.

Shawn Donnan, "Australia Tackles a Cute Conundrum," *Christian Science Monitor*, July 18, 2000.

Clyde Farnsworth, "Australia's Population Crisis: Cuddly Little Critters," *New York Times*, April 18, 1997.

Kids Discover, "Koalas and Kangaroos," January 1996.

Julie Lewis, "Driven Up a Tree," *Scientific American*, December 1999.

Roger Maynard, "Koalas to Have Pill Implant," *Times* (London), April 28, 1997.

Oliver Payne, "Koalas Out on a Limb," *National Geographic*, April 1995.

Tony Perry, "In Danger Down Under," *Los Angeles Times*, December 25, 1994.

Joni Praded, "The Koala Enigma," *Animals*, May 1999.

Ron Scherer, "Australia's Disappearing Koalas," *Christian Science Monitor*, July 1, 1997.

Ron Scherer, "Australia's French Island: Land of the Cuddly Koala," *Christian Science Monitor*, July 1, 1997.

Peter James Speilmann, "Australian Officials Consider Moving Thousands of Koalas," *Houston Chronicle*, July 26, 1997.

Gary Stix, "Broken Dreamtime: Will the Koala Go the Way of the Dodo?" *Scientific American*, February 1995.

St. Louis Post-Dispatch, "Koala Hunt Otherwise They Will Starve, Say Australian Wildlife Officers," July 5, 1996.

Elaine Stratford et al., "Managing the Koala Problem: Interdisciplinary Perspectives," *Conservation Biology*, June 2000.

Time for Kids, "The Koala Catchers: Rescuers Go Out on a Limb to Save the Furry Creatures," April 3, 1998.

Diane Toroian, "Two Koalas from Australia Have Died of Kidney Failure This Month at Zoo," *St. Louis Post-Dispatch*, July 27, 1999.

U.S. Fish and Wildlife Service, "Final Determination of Threatened Status for the Koala," *Federal Register*, May 9, 2000.

Internet Sources

Agence France-Presse, "Australian Bush Fires an Ecological Disaster, Say Fire Authorities," December 7, 1997. http://forests.org/archive/spacific/ozecodis.htm.

Mike Archer, "The Prehistory of Koalas: Apostles vs. Fossils," *Australian Skeptics*. www.skeptics.com.au/journal/koalahist.htm.

Australian Broadcasting Corporation, "Predicting Where Koalas Will Do Lunch." www.abc.net.au/science/news/print/print_119333.htm.

Australian Koala Foundation, "National Koala Act." www.savethekoala.com/nka.html.

Australian Museum Online, "Early Koala Defamed." www.austmus.gov.au/is/library/fact/koala.htm.

Richard Baker, "Too Many Koalas, So It's Time to Move On," *The Age*, May 9, 2000. www.theage.com.au/news/20000509/A49342-2000May8.html.

Jenny Bryant, "Wildlife Carer's Report," *Folklaw News*, Autumn 1998. http://home.vicnet.net.au/~folklaw/Knews~1.htm.

Pam Clunie, "How You Can Help Koalas on Private Land," Victoria Department of Natural Resources and Environment. www.nre.vic.gov.au/web/root/domino/infseries/infsheet.nsf/ec56 0317440956e24a2568e301/29/019/df659.

CNN, "Koalas Overcrowded Down Under," November 30, 1996. http://cnn.com/EARTH/9611/30/koalas/index.html.

CSIRO Plant Industry, "Growing Salinity Solutions," July 3, 2000. www.pi.csiro.au/Media/MediaRelease/MR03-07-00.htm.

Department of Agriculture, Fisheries and Forestry—Australia, "Sustainable Forest Management—Australia." www.affa.gov.au/outputs/forestry.html.

Department of Natural Resources, Queensland, "Sclerophyll Forests." www.dnr.qld.gov.au/fact_sheets/pdf_files/F06.pdf.

Environment Australia, "Action Plan for Australian Marsupials and Monotremes." www.enviornment.gov.au/threaten/plans/action/marsupials.

Environment Australia, "The Greater Blue Mountains Area, Inscribed 2000." www.environment.gov.au/heritage/awhg/whu/sites/blue.html.

Environment Victoria, "Strzelecki Conflict over Forest Clearing," www.lexicon.net/peterc/PAGES/ STRZ.HTM.

Environmental News Service, "Australia Draws Energy, Carbon, and Oil from Eucalyptus Trees," December 15, 2000. http://forests.org/archive/spacific/audrener.htm.

Friends of the Koalas, "Koala Watch Report: Status of Phillip Island's Koala Population." http://home.vicnet.net.au/~koalas/kwreport.html.

Jenny Goldie, "Australia Sets Standard for Sustainable Land Use," Environmental News Network, December 29, 2000. www.enn.com/enn-news-archive/2000/12/12292000/landcare_39459.asp.

Suzanne Herp, "Goodie Goodie Gumdrop," Australian Koala Foundation. www.akf.au/More_ Koala.html.

Amanda Hodge, "By Gum, It's Enough to Drive Them Out of Their Tree," *The Australian*. http://news.com.au/common/story_page/0,4057,1323099%5E421,00.html.

P. Menkhorst, D. Middleton, and B. Walters, "Managing Over-Abundant Koalas in Victoria." http://www.newcastle.edu.au/department/bi/birjt/marsupialcrc/marsupsymp/toomuch.html.

Natural Heritage Trust, "Bushcare." www.alga.com.au/bio2.htm.

Natural Resource Management, Commonwealth of Australia, "National Landcare Program." www.landcare.gov.au/docs/nrm/landcare/description.html.

Nature Conservation Council of New South Wales, "Land for Wildlife, Queensland." www.nccnsw.org.au/member/tsn/projects/QLD/LFW.html.

New South Wales National Parks and Wildlife Service, "Koala." www.npws.nsw.gov.au/wildlife/thr_profiles/koala.pdf.

New South Wales National Parks and Wildlife Service, "Save the Bush." www.npws.nsw.gov.au/wildlife/savebush.htm.

Reuters News Service, "Australia Criticised for Massive Tree Felling," February 22, 2000. http://forests.org/archive/spacific/aucremass.htm.

Reuters News Service, "Australia Disputes U.S. Listing Koalas as Endangered," May 20, 2000. http://forests.org/archive/ spacific/audissus.htm.

Reuters News Service, "Koala Put on U.S. Endangered Species List," May 10, 2000. http://forests.org/archive/spacific/koalapuz.htm.

Reuters News Service, "Proposal to Cull 2,000 Koalas Quashed, March 26, 1996. http://forests.org/archive/spacific/koallots.htm.

W. Robinson, "Leukemia in Koalas: The Evidence for Viral Involvement," Koalas Diseases. www.onthenet.com.au/~jbergh/koala3.htm.

Ann Sharp and Steve Phillips, "Koalas, Science, and Conservation," Australian Koala Foundation. www.akfkoala.gil.com.au/khaksc.html.

Geoff Spencer, "Kill Koalas? Controversy Engulfs 2,000 Cuddly Bears," Associated Press, March 19, 1996. http://detnews.com/menu/stories/40487.htm.

Ian Temby, "Problems Caused by Koalas," Victoria Department of Natural Resources and Environment. www.nre.vic.gov.au/web/root/domino/infseries/infsheet.nsf/5431d67568a15da64a25651903/12/01a/9a50c.

The Wilderness Society, "Key Features of South East Queensland Forest Agreement and Government Plan." www.wilderness.org.au/projects/Forests/qldaccord.html.

The Wilderness Society, "The Threats to Australia's Forests." www.wilderness.org.au/member/tws/projects/Forests/why1.htm.

James Woodford and Claire Miller, "Blue Mountains Join List of World Treasures," *Sydney Morning Herald*, November 30, 2000. http://forests.org/archive/spacific/bmjoismh.htm.

Zoological Parks and Garden Board of Victoria, "How Can I Help?: Conservation Tips." http://zoo.org.au/static/conservation/How2Help.htm.

Websites

Australian Rainforest Conservation Society, http://rainforest.org.au. This environmental group monitors and protects forests in southeastern Australia, some with koalas.

Environment Australia, www.environment.gov.au. The government agency in Australia that oversees environmental programs.

Environment Victoria, www.envict.org.au. A citizens' advocacy group trying to save wild areas in Victoria.

Friends of Local Koalas Land and Wildlife, http://homevicnet.au/~folklaw/. A group of koala advocates in Victoria.

The Greater Blue Mountains Area, www.environment.gov.au/ heritage/awhg/whu/sites/blue.html. A look at the World Heritage property protected by the UNESCO World Heritage program.

Koala Bushland Coordinated Conservation, www.env.qld.gov. au/environment/park/discover/koala.pdf. This prime koala habitat in Queensland is protected by an agreement among many owners.

Koala Conservation Center, www.penguins.org.au/koalas/pages/ page2.html. Information about the Koala Conservation Centre on Phillip Island.

Lone Pine Koala Sanctuary, www.koala.net. The first koala sanctuary opened in 1927, outside Brisbane in Queensland.

National Association of Forest Industries, www.nafi.com.au/ k12/ourforests/harvesting.html. This national organization of Australian companies involved in timber harvesting outlines its mission to promote sustainable forests.

Index

Picture Credits

Cover photo: Digital Stock
Archive Photos/Reuters/David Gray, 39
Brian Casey, 53, 54, 55, 57, 59
CORBIS/Eye Ubiquitous, 37
CORBIS/Robert Garvey, 65
CORBIS/Shai Ginott, 28
CORBIS/Kt Kittle, 61
CORBIS/Charles & Josette Lenars, 66
CORBIS/Papilio, 17
Liaison/James Pozarik, 42
North Wind Picture Archives, 29, 31
Photo Researchers, Inc./Bill Bachman, 25, 68, 72
Photo Researchers, Inc./Jen and Des Bartlett, 47
Photo Researchers, Inc./Gregory G. Dimijian, 18
Photo Researchers, Inc./Kenneth W. Fink, 20
Photo Researchers, Inc./David Hosking, 40
Photo Researchers, Inc./Joyce Photographics, 71
Photo Researchers, Inc./Tom McHugh, 23
PictureQuest/Black Star Publishing/Michael Coyne, 81
Stock Montage, Inc., 33
Zoological Society of San Diego, 7, 10, 12, 16, 21, 35, 44, 79, 87, 88, 89, 91

About the Author

Ann Malaspina has written nonfiction books for young people since 1997. This is her fourth book for Lucent Books. She has a B.A. in English from Kenyon College and an M.S. in journalism from Boston University. She lives in northern New Jersey with her family.